# Strategies for Growing and Enhancing University-Level Japanese Programs

*Strategies for Growing and Enhancing University-Level Japanese Programs* offers foreign language program managers and directors, as well as teachers of less commonly taught languages, the insights and proven practical actions they can take to enhance and grow their language programs.

Using the Japanese program at UNC Charlotte as the primary case study, author Fumie Kato provides step-by-step instructions on how she grew the Japanese program there from 133 students per semester in 2002 to 515 students per semester in 2017; from a program with just one full-time professor and one part-time faculty member, to a faculty of seven full-time and three part-time members.

While Japanese is the example used in the book, the principles can be applied by anyone managing foreign language/less commonly taught language programs who wishes to expand their program and raise their students' success rates. The book is therefore of interest to instructors, coordinators and directors of foreign language education programs throughout the world.

**Fumie Kato** is Associate Professor of Japanese at the University of North Carolina at Charlotte, USA. Her expertise lies in applied linguistics, specifically foreign language acquisition, learning strategies, student motivation and PBLL (Project-Based Language Learning). She earned a PhD in applied linguistics at the University of Sydney in 2001. She moved to Charlotte as an assistant professor in 2004. She has received five prestigious awards: International Education Faculty Award; finalist, Bank of America Award for Teaching Excellence; Bonnie Cone Early-Career Professorship in Teaching Award; AATJ's (American Association of Teachers of Japanese) 2016 Teacher Award; Foreign Minister's Commendations in Honor of the 70th Anniversary of the End of the War with the United States of America, as well as many competitive grants. Dr. Kato's publications include *Improving Student Motivation toward Japanese Learning* (2010), written in English and Japanese from Gakujutsu Shuppansha in Japan, and more than 15 peer-reviewed articles in journals including *Language Teaching Research* and *Foreign Language Annals*. She has developed approximately ten courses and redesigned seven others for the Japanese Program at UNC Charlotte, which offers a translation certificate, graduate translation certificate, business certificate and a Japanese BA Honors degree.

**Ryan Spring** is Associate Professor at the Institute for Excellence in Higher Education at Tohoku University, Japan. He received a PhD in language communication from the Graduate School of International Culture Studies at the same university in 2014. He has published a number of papers in journals such as *Cognitive Linguistics* and *Foreign Language Annals* and is an active member of conferences such as the English Linguistic Society of Japan and the Association for Teaching English through Multimedia, where he serves as vice president of the East Japan branch. He has also received several awards for both education and research, including winning the Tohoku University President's Award, once for each area, and the 2017 Contribution to Education Award, as well as a number of competitive grants from the Japan Society for the Promotion of Science. Dr. Spring is currently working on curriculum reform at Tohoku University, and helps with graduate courses and the development of language and culture programs such as faculty-led study abroad trips.

# Strategies for Growing and Enhancing University-Level Japanese Programs

Fumie Kato
Edited by Ryan Spring

LONDON AND NEW YORK

First published 2020
by Routledge
2 Park Square, Milton Park, Abingdon, Oxon OX14 4RN

and by Routledge
52 Vanderbilt Avenue, New York, NY 10017

*Routledge is an imprint of the Taylor & Francis Group, an informa business*

© 2020 Fumie Kato

The right of Fumie Kato to be identified as author of this work has been asserted by her in accordance with sections 77 and 78 of the Copyright, Designs and Patents Act 1988.

All rights reserved. No part of this book may be reprinted or reproduced or utilised in any form or by any electronic, mechanical, or other means, now known or hereafter invented, including photocopying and recording, or in any information storage or retrieval system, without permission in writing from the publishers.

*Trademark notice*: Product or corporate names may be trademarks or registered trademarks, and are used only for identification and explanation without intent to infringe.

*British Library Cataloguing-in-Publication Data*
A catalogue record for this book is available from the British Library

*Library of Congress Cataloging-in-Publication Data*
Names: Kato, Fumie, author. | Spring, Ryan E., editor.
Title: Strategies for growing and enhancing university-level Japanese programs / Fumie Kato, Ryan E. Spring (editor).
Description: 1. | New York : Routledge, 2020. |
Includes bibliographical references and index.
Identifiers: LCCN 2019046174 (print) | LCCN 2019046175 (ebook) | ISBN 9780367373856 (hardback) | ISBN 9780367373849 (paperback) | ISBN 9780429353451 (ebook)
Subjects: LCSH: Japanese language–Study and teaching (Higher) | Second language acquisition–Study and teaching (Higher) | Language and languages–Study and teaching (Higher)
Classification: LCC PL519 .K373 2020 (print) | LCC PL519 (ebook) | DDC 495.680071/1–dc23
LC record available at https://lccn.loc.gov/2019046174
LC ebook record available at https://lccn.loc.gov/2019046175

ISBN: 978-0-367-37385-6 (hbk)
ISBN: 978-0-367-37384-9 (pbk)
ISBN: 978-0-429-35345-1 (ebk)

Typeset in Palatino LT Std
by Newgen Publishing UK

# Contents

| | |
|---|---|
| *List of figures* | vi |
| *List of tables* | vii |
| *Preface* | ix |
| *Acknowledgement* | xi |
| Introduction | 1 |
| 1  Utilizing technology to create opportunity and interest | 12 |
| 2  Educational strategies | 31 |
| 3  Utilizing peer teaching and tutoring to decrease attrition rates | 53 |
| 4  Study abroad opportunities: Sending and receiving | 74 |
| 5  Growing interest through extracurricular activities | 93 |
| Conclusion and recommendations | 101 |
| Postscript | 105 |
| *References* | 107 |
| *Index* | 115 |

# Figures

| | | |
|---|---|---|
| 0.1 | Overall structure | 11 |
| 1.1 | Title page: "UNCC Tohoku" website | 25 |
| 1.2 | Contents: UNC Charlotte | 25 |
| 1.3 | Contents: Tohoku University | 26 |
| 1.4 | On-campus dining at UNC Charlotte | 26 |

# Tables

| | | |
|---|---|---|
| 2.1 | Class schedule in inter-collaborative peer learning course in spring 2019 | 36 |
| 2.2 | The schedule of the collaborative project in the former half of the semester | 36 |
| 2.3 | The schedule of the five sessions for debate activity | 38 |
| 3.1 | Peer tutor list in a designated website with example entry | 66 |
| 4.1 | Study abroad student participation numbers in the Japanese program at UNC Charlotte | 83 |
| 5.1 | Semester-end presentations program | 95 |

# Preface

It was 17 years ago that I began teaching in the Japanese program at UNC Charlotte. When I think back to those early days, I realize now that I was really feeling my way around in the dark, doing things in part because I did not know in detail about the organization of universities in the United States and simply trying to do my best to clear up the work and duties in front of my face, one by one. I have worked as a language instructor for most of my life and approximately half of my career has been dedicated to UNC Charlotte.

It has been extremely inspiring to me to know that the outcomes of my teaching history at UNC Charlotte have been so meaningful: the numbers of students, courses, Japanese majors, graduates in Japanese majors, and teachers have successfully grown to four or five times what they were when I started teaching at UNC Charlotte in 2002. In addition, according to the *Chronicle of Higher Education* January edition of 2019, the number of graduates in Japanese language majors at our university was the fourth in the United States, following only universities in Hawaii and Los Angeles, whose environments, that is, many opportunities to use the Japanese language, several Japanese companies and tourists, ensure high enrollment rates. The news of this amazed not only instructors in the Japanese program but also those of all the other foreign language programs and officials at UNC Charlotte. They could hardly believe that Japanese, which they considered to be such a minor foreign language in the southeastern region of the United States, was ranked in the top level in the United States! I surely couldn't have imagined or expected that we would grow as much as we did 17 years ago.

I repeatedly mention in my book how difficult it is to promote foreign language learning in areas where the target language is minor. It is not uncommon for students whose first languages are European to discontinue studying Japanese, which is one of the hardest foreign languages for them to learn, if there is no incentive and if we just teach language without taking any action to integrate strategies into our courses. Based on my teaching policies acquired through my PhD research, that is, how to prevent students from withdrawing or failing courses, and how to improve students' motivation levels, I have incorporated numerous teaching strategies into our courses, curriculum and in extracurricular activities for these 17 years. I feel that the report in the *Chronicle of Higher Education* (Chronicle List, 2019) legitimizes the strategies that I integrated into the Japanese program and helps verify how effective and efficient they were.

I wrote this book with the hope that other minor foreign language instructors might utilize some of the same strategies that I put into effect in my Japanese program, and that they will be equally useful, helpful and beneficial for them. I encourage not only classroom instructors but also course coordinators, curriculum developers and researchers in the world who have to deal with the problems related to teaching a minor foreign language to read the book and integrate some of these strategies into their own institutions. About a half of the research studies including in this book were accepted and published by various journals as research studies, where they were accepted as having contributed to the field of foreign language teaching. As only summaries of the outcomes of these strategies are included in my book, if you are interested in more detailed descriptions, please read the original research manuscripts for more in depth comprehensive research reports. Additionally, I provided teachers with practical advice for incorporating the strategies described in this book into their institutions, so please take note of this advice as well. I sincerely hope that readers of my book will implement some strategies in their own language courses, programs or institutions and be successful in improving their students' motivation levels to be able to continue learning their target languages, to overcome some obstacles until they have achieved their goals, and to ultimately develop solid foreign language education programs.

# Acknowledgement

Publishing of this book was supported in part by fund from Japan Foundation.

# Introduction

## 0.1 What is a minor foreign language?

Much of the research surrounding foreign language (henceforth, FL) learning and second language (henceforth, L2) acquisition tend to focus on the general process of acquiring a new language, sometimes painting learners with the same brush. However, while some of the challenges and problems that learners of different languages face are similar (i.e., memorizing new vocabulary, problems with pronunciation, etc.), others are specific to the target-first language pair (depending on how typologically similar the two languages are), and many still are unique to the environment in which the students are learning. This is the very reason that a distinction is made between FL learning (studying a language other than the first language in circumstances where the language is not used in the surrounding environment) and L2 learning (studying a language other than one's first language in circumstances where the target language is primarily used).

As indicated by a large number of researchers (e.g., Rubin & Thompson, 1994; Scarcella & Oxford, 1992; Tung, 1998; Varner & Palmer, 2002), L2 learners often progress more quickly and achieve higher levels of proficiency than FL learners because of more input, interaction with, immersion in, and time spent practicing the TL (henceforth, TL). However, much less attention has been drawn to the differences in FLs based on how prevalent they are in the surrounding community. Just as there is a difference in how much interaction L2 learners and FL learners have with their TLs, the amount of opportunities to use, practice and come into authentic contact with the TL is vastly different for major FLs (ones that are somewhat established in the surrounding community) and minor FLs (ones that are under-represented in the surrounding community). For example, in the state of Texas, Spanish would be considered a major FL because though it is not the primary or official language of the state, there are a number of Spanish speakers and Spanish-language radio stations, newspapers, restaurants in the community. Thus, if one were to attempt to learn Spanish in Texas, there would be abundant opportunities to interact in the TL. However, the same cannot be said if one were to attempt to learn a minor foreign language such as French in Japan, or German in Brazil. It is this difference in opportunity that sets minor and major FLs apart, and creates special challenges for educators of minor FLs.

## 0.2 What are the specific challenges that minor foreign language programs face?

The first and most arduous problem that learners and educators of minor FLs have is a poverty of opportunity. With L2 learning, and to a lesser degree major FL learning, there are abundant opportunities outside the class-hours to practice reading, writing, listening and speaking the TL and utilizing the related skills learned in the classroom. L2 learners have more chances to use the explicit knowledge learned in the classroom in their daily lives, by which they internalize it and make more gains in implicit knowledge. For example, L2 learners can find friends and build relationships with native speakers using their L2, which is argued to be one of the more effective methods to learn a new language (Rubin & Thompson, 1994; Scarcella & Oxford, 1992). However, finding a close friend is, regrettably, not something everyone can do, even if they work hard at it, and this only becomes more difficult when the pool of candidates is smaller, as it is for learners of minor FLs. For these learners, even though they may want to speak their TL, if there are very few native speakers around them, there are not many opportunities to listen to, read, or interact with their target FL, and they must therefore redouble their efforts just to attempt to use the language. Thus, compared to L2 learners, there are far fewer chances in their daily lives to use the TL, practice, and internalize explicit knowledge acquired through study.

The second problem that minor FL educators often face is a poverty of interest. Students often see the potential in studying major FLs, as they perceive them as potentially useful in daily-life situations or their future careers. If the FL is well represented in the surrounding environment, they are sent a clear message that there is a large community that uses the language, and thus there is a greater chance that they will have higher instrumental motivation (desire to accomplish a task, such as getting a certificate or a better job [Gardner & Lambert, 1972; Hernández, 2010]) to learn the language. However, minor FLs are by definition not well represented in the surrounding community, and thus learners are often less motivated to learn the language as they may not see the point in it because there is no clear use for it in their daily lives or immediate future. This lack of motivation is especially troublesome because students require it when they encounter obstacles in their learning, which is, unfortunately, somewhat unavoidable when learning a FL. When students begin to feel frustrated with the difficulties of their TL, they often leave or withdraw from classes (Kato, 2000). This can cause extra problems for educators, as many times the existence of FL programs depends entirely on the number of students taking classes and the amount of interest garnered in the language. For example, in North Carolina in the United States, where Japanese is a minor FL, there is difficulty getting students to join classes and even more to get them to continue studying it, which has resulted in many universities and high schools in the area downsizing the number of classes and laying off teachers. This threat has been looming in recent times as colleges across the United States have shut down 651 FL programs over the last three years (Johnson, 2019). While the fear of losing funding, jobs, and programs is very real for all FL educators, these problems affect minor FLs disproportionally, as the problems mentioned above can make keeping students in especially difficult for these programs.

## 0.3 Combatting these challenges by increasing motivation

The best way for educators to solve both the poverty of opportunity and poverty of interest that minor FL learners face is to increase their motivation. First of all, increased motivation means more interest, which attracts students and ensures the existence and continuation of minor FL programs and classes. While some may think motivation can be easily increased through simple means, such as sharing pop-media or fun activities, it is not easy to keep students' interest piqued. Simply doing one fun activity might initially attract interest, but it will surely not keep them interested for years to come so that students continue to take classes and reach their language proficiency goals, and improperly motivated students often withdraw from classes and programs when they reach higher levels where they have to learn more difficult concepts and acquire more linguistic structures and advanced vocabulary.

Furthermore, motivation is often touted as one of the most important student variables in language learning (Oxford & Shearin, 1996) and the best predictor of the rate and success of L2/FL acquisition, as well as student achievement and academic performance (Gardner, 1985; Oxford, Park-Oh, Ito, & Sumrall, 1993; Pintrich, Smith, Garcia, & Mckeachie, 1993; Samimy & Tabuse, 1992). Gardner (2001) indicates, "[motivation is] a central element … in determining success in learning another language in the classroom setting" (p. 3). Dörnyei (2001a) notes that "99 per cent of language learners who really want to learn a FL (i.e., who are really motivated) will be able to master a reasonable working knowledge of it" (p. 2). Therefore, it has often been suggested that educators should strive to maximize student motivation (MacIntyre, Noels, & Clément, 1997; Samimy & Tabuse, 1992). Although Gardner (2001) admits that the "major contributors to language learning motivation is first and foremost the student" (p. 17), he also notes that it is influenced by their backgrounds and teachers, who have a major role in motivating students.

Dörney (2001a) further examines the differences in types of motivation. He defined the notable distinction between *intrinsic* motivation, that is, performing to experience pleasure and satisfaction for the joy of doing a particular activity, and *extrinsic* motivation, that is, performing to receive some reward or to avoid punishment. Highly motivated FL/L2 students are said to learn languages for their internal satisfaction (Dörnyei, 2001a; Ehrman, 1996). Therefore, many argue that intrinsic motivation is the most powerful and important type in FL/L2 learning (Oxford et al., 1993). Dörnyei (2001a) also notes that motivation may be positive or negative. While intrinsic motivation is generally positive and increases learner performance, too much extrinsic motivation can become negatively motivating, causing anxiety which "interferes with [students'] ability to use their skills and abilities" (Ehrman, 1996, p. 138). In fact, there is a significant negative correlation between language anxiety and language performance and too much anxiety has been found to result in lower grades (Aida, 1994; Gardner, 2001; Kato, 2000; MacIntyre & Gardners, 1994; MacIntyre et al., 1997; Oxford, 1999; Saito & Samimy, 1996). Therefore, it is crucial for teachers of minor FLs to provide learners with an enjoyable and anxiety-free environment for learning in order to enhance student motivation levels.

My primary teaching strategy has thus been to devise ways for students to learn their TL easily and enjoyably with minimal anxiety. Likewise, my research has been focused on creating effective strategies to counteract the problems that many minor FL teachers encounter, such as the poverty of opportunity and the poverty of interest, by increasing intrinsic student motivation. While at the University of Sydney, I worked to introduce and examine the effectiveness of learning strategies, time management, and anxiety-free learning in basic Japanese (Kato, 2000). Although the English native speakers there, that is, Australian students in Sydney, decided to study Japanese and register for Japanese language courses, around half of them withdrew from every class before it concluded or received an F. According to Saito and Samimy (1996), the attrition rate among students studying Japanese has been reported to be as much as 80%. Their results shocked me, as did the high attrition rates in my own courses when I first began teaching. Because these students decided to challenge themselves by studying and learning a language as difficult as Japanese, I wanted them to see it through until the end of the semester. Therefore, I made the primary purpose of my research to figure out what teaching methods would be effective in this respect, and approached this problem from an applied linguistics and FL acquisition standpoint.

My second key strategy, related to managing courses has been to encourage registered students not to give up or withdraw during their studies. This book was written to show some of the strategies and approaches I have successfully implemented as a minor FL educator to increase participation in my program and heighten intrinsic student motivation, and provide valuable opportunities to my students to interact authentically with their TL. These approaches are all helpful to alleviate both the poverty of opportunity and poverty of interest problems that most minor FL learners and educators face. They are discussed in the context of my own experiences and an overarching case study of teaching Japanese in the southeastern part of the United States but can easily be adapted and utilized by any FL educator, regardless of the area or TL. These strategies have been proven effective in my own university, where I integrated them into our program in order to strengthen student motivation and grow our university-level Japanese program from a nearly extinct program into the fourth largest in the country, placed only behind top-ranking universities where Japanese is not considered a minor FL.

## 0.4 The case of Japanese at the University of North Carolina at Charlotte

In 2002, after obtaining my postgraduate education from the University of Sydney, where I had previously also taught Japanese, I moved to Charlotte, North Carolina, which is located in the southeastern region of the United States. The University of North Carolina at Charlotte (henceforth, UNC Charlotte) is the only higher academic institution in the city that offers courses in Japanese, a minor FL in the area. At the time, there was only one assistant professor working in the Japanese program. I took a part-time position teaching there but found myself with the only full-time Japanese teaching position due to my predecessor's resignation, the following semester, with only one adjunct lecturer to help me. At the time, the Department of Languages and Culture Studies in the College of Liberal Arts and Sciences offered baccalaureate degrees in Spanish, French and German. My predecessor established the Japanese program with around 40 students in 1995, shortly after which a Japanese minor degree was offered. When I started in 2002, Japanese ranked fourth (approximately 130 students per semester) in enrollment, after the aforementioned three languages. The Japanese program offered six classes in total, three elementary classes, two intermediate classes and one upper-intermediate class per semester. In addition to these FLs, the department also offered Russian, Italian, Latin, Portuguese, Arabic and Chinese (and still does).

UNC Charlotte is one of a generation of universities that were founded in various metropolitan areas of the United States immediately after World War II in response to rising education demands generated by the war and its technology. As of 2018, the university is comprised of seven professional colleges with more than 1,000 full-time faculty members and over 30,000 students. The city of Charlotte is located in North Carolina, on the east coast, in the southeastern region in the United States. Spanish is the most mainstream FL here, and boasts the largest number of registered students. Regionally, there is a large Spanish-speaking population, with many Spanish communities and social activities, and there are even local newspapers published in Spanish. This atmosphere inherently raises the instrumental (see Section 0.2) and integrative motivation (desire to become part of a TL community) (Ehrman, 1996; Gardner & Lambert, 1972) for Spanish-language learners in the area, so it is understandable that many students decide to study Spanish at UNC Charlotte.

When my predecessor left, I suddenly became the head of the entire Japanese program, which was a bit daunting at first. Japanese is a mainstream FL in Australia, where I taught before, and almost all major universities in the country have Japanese Departments. In contrast, Japanese is a minor FL in Charlotte, and when I started teaching there, it had a teaching staff of only two, with only six courses offered, so I worried about my ability to keep the program from collapsing. The universities I had taught at previously had Japanese departments with long histories and large faculties. Therefore, I had always had to put my own methods and strategies aside, and teach in a manner that aligned with that of the senior faculty members and the policies of the departments. Looking back now, the small size of the program and the circumstances were truly fortunate, because I could teach Japanese following my own teaching philosophies, and put the FL pedagogies which I learned about through my doctorate research into practice. Although apprehensive about the task at hand, I decided that my first step would be to build a firm foundation for the Japanese program.

## 0.5 Background of Japanese learning and the circumstances in Charlotte

Recently, the number of educational institutions, teachers and learners of Japanese as a FL (henceforth, JFL) have increased dramatically, although this is not true across all regions. According to the Japan Foundation's report (2017), over the last 30 years the number of institutions, teachers and learners has increased each decade, 14.1 times, 15.6 times and 28.7 times, respectively. At the time of the report, Japanese language education was being carried out in 130 countries and 7 regions other than Japan, with approximately 3.6 million students, although these numbers do not include those studying Japanese through television, radio, the Internet, or private lessons. However, according to data from 2012, the number of JFL educational institutions and teachers had decreased by around 8.2% in North America, the only area that saw such trends (Rollins, 2015). Part of the reason for this could be due to the highlighting of Chinese as a FL in the United States due to China's powerful economic status in the past two decades. Although Chinese classes have been increasing in the United States, JFL here has recently faced reductions in numbers of classes, students and programs. This has been felt in my region as well, where a few years ago I received an email from a high school teacher in North Carolina who asked me to support her by writing a letter to the North Carolina Education Board on her behalf because her Japanese classes faced the possibility of termination due to their policy of decreasing language classes in the state. One of the reasons for the decline of JFL in the Charlotte regional area is probably due to the fact that Japanese is a very minor FL for the area. Every time I would hear about what other JFL teachers in my area were going through, it made me strive harder to increase, or at least maintain, the number of students studying Japanese at my own institution.

Japanese's status as a minor FL is also due in part to the history of Charlotte, being founded largely in part by German immigrants, which is evidenced by the fact that the city and surrounding county were named in honor of German princess Charlotte of Mecklenburg-Strelitz. The large German influence in Charlotte continues to this day as the largest population of foreign residents in Charlotte is still German, and the largest percentage of foreign owned companies in the city are also German, followed by companies from the United Kingdom, Canada and then Japan. In contrast, there is only one language academy where immersion courses are offered in Japanese, as well as in French, German, and Chinese. Japanese courses are offered in only a few middle and high schools and in only one higher education institution, UNC Charlotte. My predecessor also opened a Japanese program at a private university in Charlotte, but it closed only a few years later.

The low number of Japanese residents in Charlotte also helps to place Japanese as a minor FL in the region. In 2018, US Census Bureau estimated the population of North Carolina was 10 million, and the population of Charlotte itself was 872,498, making it the largest city in North Carolina. However, according to the data by Consulate General of Japan in Atlanta, the number of Japanese residents in the city was only 7,000, and Japanese tourists are rarely seen in Charlotte. It is thus quite rare for US students to meet Japanese people or come in contact with the Japanese language outside of their classes. This means that even if students learn Japanese for a few years at UNC Charlotte, they may graduate from the university having had only little contact with Japanese natives other than their instructors. Also, even if they graduate, it is quite difficult to find local jobs where they can make use of their Japanese language abilities. Because of these circumstances, Japanese is seen as a language that does not have much impact on students' lives outside the university. Students sometimes lament that when they tell their friends that they study Japanese, their friends often ask them why they chose to study it. Unfortunately, this is not a rare comment.

## 0.6 Particular problems for JFL learners in Charlotte

As mentioned in previous sections, minor FL learners often suffer from a poverty of opportunity, and this is no different for JFL learners in Charlotte and the southeast of the United States in general. There are several opportunities for Spanish learners in Charlotte to read local newspapers published in Spanish, visit Spanish communities, and participate in local Spanish-speaking events. Furthermore, if students master Spanish, there are a number of companies and job opportunities in the greater area that reward Spanish proficiency, and it can greatly increase their chances in the job market postgraduation. German learners in the area also have similar opportunities and extrinsically motivating factors, while Japanese learners in Charlotte have far fewer. Although Japanese is not considered a minor FL in some parts of the United States (e.g., Honolulu, Los Angeles, and New York), in the southeastern region it is very minor, with none of the advantages of major FLs.

JFL education in the Charlotte region suffers not only because Japanese is considered a very minor FL in the area but also because it is such a difficult language for native English speakers to learn. It belongs to a different family of languages than English, which makes it typologically different on almost every measurable linguistic scale from morphology, syntax and semantics (Tsunoda, 2009) to more abstract measures such as cognitive and social linguistics (e.g., Hinds, 1987; Spring & Horie, 2013). These differences present a number of challenges to students that can quickly demotivate them and cause them to withdraw or give up. For example, while English shares many similar words with many other European languages, it shares hardly any with Japanese, necessitating the learning of a large number of words with completely different origins as well as the characters. The syntactic, semantic and phonetic differences make it difficult as well. For example, the grammatical structures of the two languages are completely different, English being predominantly SVO in structure and Japanese being SOV in structure (Tsunoda, 2009), which causes a number of other difficulties in learning the language such as differences in where relative clause is placed, question word fronting, verb placement and grammatical marking placements. In terms of pronunciation, Japanese and English are also different, with English being considered a stress-timed language and Japanese being considered either a syllable-timed or mora-timed language (Dauer, 1983; Ladefoged, 1975), which causes problems for learners as well. Furthermore, the semantic and cognitive patterns in the two languages are also different, with Japanese being verb-framed and English being satellite-framed, which affects focus and the standard patterns for event descriptions (Spring & Horie, 2013).

Another reason why the Japanese language is so difficult for native English speakers to master is that it uses a completely different writing system from the Western European alphabet. Therefore, there is an additional burden in acquiring reading and writing skills, as students must learn two phonetic syllabaries, that is, Hiragana and Katakana (55 characters each), and at least 300 kanji characters (ideograms adapted from Chinese, consisting of large number of strokes) with 160 sets of kanji compounds, which presents a formidable challenge to native English learners. Learning these written symbols requires an enormous amount of effort, especially when considering that for full mastery of Japanese, a total of approximately 2,000 kanji characters is required (Japan Agency for Cultural Affairs, 2010).

Because the Japanese and English languages are entirely different in terms of characters, words, pronunciation, sentence structure, grammar and more, it is recognized as being one of the most difficult FLs to master for native speakers of English. To achieve useful basic proficiency such as level 3 in it and other character-based languages, an average of 2,400 to 2,700 contact hours is required, as compared with the 720 need to reach the same level for the major European languages (Liskin-Gasparro, 1982). Therefore, Japanese is classified as a category IV language in terms of degree of difficulty for native speakers of English (Jordan & Lambert, 1991), and it is recognized as much more difficult to learn than various European languages, that is, it takes 3–4 times more time and effort.

## 0.7 Strategies to enhance student motivation presented in this book

As argued in Section 0.3, the most important aspect of overcoming the challenges that learners and educators of minor FLs face is to increase student motivation, and this is no different for the JFL learners in Charlotte. While it is challenging to promote the learning of a minor FL, during my tenure as the coordinator of the Japanese program at UNC Charlotte for the past 17 years, I have employed the strategies introduced in this book to great success. During this time, the program saw dramatic increases in the number of learners (133/semester in 2002 to 501/semester in 2018), courses offered (6 in 2002 to 25 in 2018), instructors (from 2 to 10), students who study abroad (from 4 in 2002 to 30 in 2018), and students who majoring (0 in 2002 to 146 in 2018) and minoring (36 in 2002 to 73 in 2018) in Japanese. These strategies boosted Japanese to the FL program with the second most registered students and major degrees at UNC Charlotte, following only Spanish, despite being a minor FL. Furthermore, according to the *Chronicle of Higher Education* (January 29, 2019), UNC Charlotte ranked number four in number of degrees awarded in Japanese amongst private and public higher education institutions in 2016–2017, only behind much larger universities in Hawaii and California, where Japanese is a major FL.

This book presents several of the strategies that I have implemented in the Japanese program at UNC Charlotte to overcome the poverty of opportunity and poverty of interest problems my students of Japanese experienced. Chapter 1 and Sections 2.2, 3.2 and 4.2 of Chapters 2, 3 and 4 focus on the strategies providing students with opportunities to communicate with Japanese native speaking students. They describe the theoretical framework of the strategies (i.e., the social constructivist theory of learning and motivation types in FL learning), procedures for integration, and analysis of the outcomes of each. Finally, two representative extra-curricular activities that have been integrated into the Japanese program are presented in Chapter 5. This book is written in the context of using such teaching approaches to improve student motivation, and although it uses teaching Japanese at UNC Charlotte as its central case study, the approaches and strategies herein are applicable to all minor FLs.

One important and effective way to help minor FL learners is to increase study abroad opportunities. While this may seem obvious, most people forget that the reason for doing this is not only to send learners, but also to receive them. For example, in the case of UNC Charlotte, increased study abroad rates have not only afforded our students with valuable experiences but have also increased the number of incoming Japanese university students, which naturally increases the opportunities for minor FL learners to interact with native speakers, and also opens up a number of opportunities for collaborative learning, advanced programs and innovative classes. Now that UNC Charlotte has many Japanese study abroad students, we can invite them to classes and to Japanese-related events and student organizations. Thus, the more foreign students that come to one's institution, the more possibilities and options one has for helping their minor FL students. In fact, some of the strategies in this book are only feasible with some degree of foreign students at one's institution, so if there are currently few at your own institution, I highly recommend doing what you can to increase these numbers. However, I also recognize that readers will have various levels of incoming students currently at their institution. I could not have even implemented some of these strategies myself when I first took my position at UNC Charlotte. Therefore, I have created the following guide, which can help other minor FL educators select strategies from the book that might be best suited to their current needs.

1. For institutions with very few incoming foreign student native speakers or exchange partners, the strategies containing VSCMC (Chapter 1), self-assessment (Chapter 2), peer tutoring (Chapter 3) and growing interest (Chapter 5) will be most applicable.
2. For institutions with low to medium numbers, the LA Program (Chapter 3) and Short-Term Visiting Program (Chapter 4) may be most applicable, in addition to the previous strategies.
3. For institutions with high (or increasing) numbers, the Inter-Collaborative Peer Learning strategy (Chapter 2) can also be used.

Figure 0.1 shows the overall structure of this book, where the specific problems that minor FL students and teachers face are specifically addressed herein, and how the strategies outlined in each chapter address them.

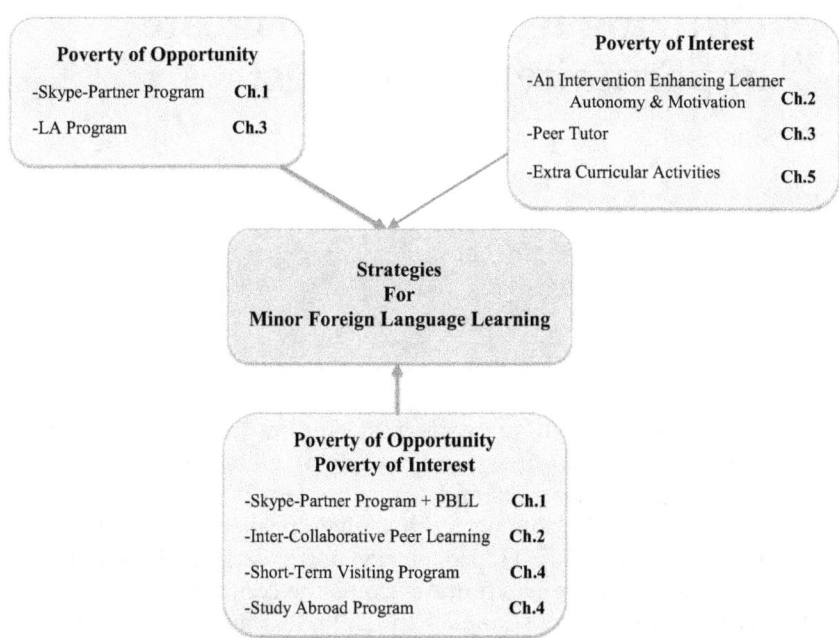

*Figure 0.1* Overall structure.

It should be noted that the strategies introduced in this book are completely applicable to any FL. Although they are framed within the case study of teaching Japanese at UNC Charlotte, any of them can be used regardless of what the FL and area is. The last part of each section and the conclusion provide practical advice for teachers of (minor) FLs who want to utilize the strategies with their students, grow their own programs, improve student learning, or help students overcome the problems of poverty of opportunity and poverty of interest.

# 1 Utilizing technology to create opportunity and interest

## 1.1 Introduction

This chapter presents two strategies that employ the Internet to overcome the poverty of opportunity and poverty of interest that many minor foreign language (FL) learners and educators face by allowing students chances to authentically interact with native speakers. These strategies also help students develop TL proficiency, particularly oral communication skills. A wealth of research underscores the contribution interacting with a native speaker of a TL makes to L2/FL learners' proficiency (e.g., Ellis, 1985; Rubin & Thompson, 1994; Scarcella & Oxford, 1992). According to the social constructivist theory of learning, individuals construct knowledge through direct interactions with their social and physical environments and through reflection on those experiences (Beckett & Slater, 2005; Dooly & Sadler, 2016; Forester & Meyer, 2015; Gergen, 1999; Pardjono, 2002; Vygotzky, 1978). Following this, L2/FL instructors can seek to create learning environments in which learners can gain knowledge of their TL and culture through direct, personal interactions (Canale & Swain, 1980). The creation of these environments promotes speaking and language acquisition as it allows uninhibited practice and the performance of a range of speech acts, both of which are imperative for rapid development of L2/FL ability (Ellis, 1985). Including native speakers in these environments is important, because Scarcella and Oxford (1992) indicate that speaking with others who have more linguistic resources than the learners is essential for L2/FL development. However, providing students of minor FLs with opportunities to speak and listen can be especially difficult (Blake, 2008; Towndrow & Vallance, 2004).

The studies presented in this chapter are done so in the context of students learning Japanese in the United States and students learning English in Japan. They specifically sought to document the extent to which such learning experiences can be provided over the Internet and examine how meaningful the interactions would be and what impacts they had on the speaking abilities of both groups of learners. The two strategies introduced herein were integrated throughout the semester in two different Japanese courses in 2015 and 2017 at UNC Charlotte. The first was the creation of a video-synchronous computer-mediated communication (henceforth, VSCMC) learning program (Skype partner program) with Japanese students from a partner university (Tohoku University) into oral communication classes for mutually beneficial learning. The second is the integration of project-based language learning into the existing program to enhance student motivation levels and inter-partner communication. Advice for instructors who might want to create similar programs at their own institutions is then offered in the final section.

## 1.2 Tackling the poverty of opportunity problem through VSCMC learning programs

VSCMC programs can theoretically help overcome the poverty of opportunity that minor FL learners face and improve oral communication skills, which is particularly difficult for learners of minor FL learners. Although there are a number of benefits to practicing with native speaking peers (Rubin & Thompson, 1994; Scarcella & Oxford, 1992), creating such opportunities for learners of minor FLs has been a challenge for instructors in the past, but new technologies such as VSCMC systems and social networking services have made such interactions much easier. However, getting partners for learners to speak with can still be challenging. If an institution has study abroad or research exchange partners abroad, these relationships can be utilized to help create such programs, as in the case of UNC Charlotte and Tohoku University, as reported throughout this chapter.

### 1.2.1 The theoretical motivation for VSCMC with native speakers

Ellis (1985) has shown that both the quantity and quality of input that L2/FL learners receive greatly impacts acquisition, and suggests that creating opportunities for more and higher quality input will aid in the successful acquisition of a L2/FL. Collaborative learning activities such as paired conversations promote cooperation among students, pushing them to work together to achieve their learning goals, which creates a lot of output and input for all parties involved. Accordingly, a number of studies that report on creating speaking opportunities for FL learners through the use of technology that allows FL learners to converse with native speakers have boasted various degrees of success (e.g., Entzinger, Morimura, & Suzuki, 2013; Kato, Spring, & Mori, 2016; Taillefer & Munoz-Luna, 2014; Tian & Wang, 2010; Yang, Gamble, & Tang, 2012). Such studies have investigated the use of VSCMC and/or voice-over instant messaging tools to facilitate FL learning using a variety of materials and research methods. However, one significant problem that arises in the body of literature is that though these studies generally suggest that providing opportunities for meaningful communication is important, there is a lack of consensus as to what actually constitutes a meaningful interaction. The theory of social constructivism, on which many VSCMC studies are based, relies heavily not just on interactions, but also on meaningful interactions, and the careful consideration of the types of interactions that are being provided is important for increased learning (Woo & Reeves, 2006). In other words, if an interaction is not meaningful, it will not benefit learning. Scarcella and Oxford (1992) also noted that opportunities for "language-promoting interaction" (p. 153) are required for developing speaking abilities. Here, the criteria vital for creating meaningful interactions can be useful in determining if the interactions would provide enough quality input to impact L2 acquisition:

1  a high quantity of input directed at the learner
2  the learner's perceived need to communicate in the L2
3  independent control of the propositional content by the learner
4  adherence to the "here and now" principle, at least initially
5  the performance of a range of speech acts by both the native speaker/ teacher and the learner
6  exposure to a high quantity of directives
7  exposure to a high quantity of "extending" utterances
8  opportunities for uninhibited "practice" (Ellis, 1985, p. 161)

I created the first VSCMC program for mutually beneficial language exchange with my colleagues and our partner university based on these ideas, and we called it the UNC Charlotte–Tohoku University Skype partner program. The main goal of the first rendition of the program was to engage participants in meaningful communication by allowing them both free and structures conversations (about assigned topics) with a native speaker of their TL, thereby promoting high-quality input where the learners were in control of the content and would participate in a range of speech acts, thus meeting many of the requirements for meaningful interaction suggested by Ellis (1985), Scarcella and Oxford (1992), and Woo and Reeves (2006). My colleagues and I also took objective FL speaking proficiency data from standardized pre- and posttests, and collected qualitative data to monitor motivation and student opinions toward the program. Our first study (Kato et al., 2016) specifically examined the following questions: (1) How does the VSCMC approach with native speakers improve their interpersonal oral abilities? and (2) Does the approach enable educators to provide learners with meaningful interactions?

### 1.2.2 A case study of a Skype partner program

We created the program with students enrolled at UNC Charlotte and Tohoku University and took data from the participants as well as a comparison group of other students enrolled at the universities who were in the same or similar classes but did not participate in the program. Taking data in this manner allowed us to test the effectiveness of the program on two parameters: how effective it was at improving learners' FL oral abilities and how meaningful interactions were.

*1.2.2.1 Participants*

The first rendition of the program consisted of four groups of students: an experimental and a comparison groups at UNC Charlotte, and an experimental and a comparison groups at Tohoku University. The US experimental group ($n = 26$) was enrolled in a "Japanese Oral Communication" class (3 credit hours) in the 2015 spring semester and students were required to participate in the Skype activity discussed in Section 1.2.2.2. They had studied Japanese for between one and a half to three years, and their oral abilities were considered to be elementary-mid to intermediate-mid level on the basis of the Oral Proficiency Interview made by the American Council on the Teaching of Foreign Languages (ACTFL). The US comparison group ($n = 12$) consisted of students with similar Japanese learning length and similar Japanese language abilities and were paid to complete pre- and posttests of oral ability. These students were still learners of Japanese, but did not enroll in the "Japanese Oral Communication" class, instead taking other Japanese language courses and various courses related to Japan such as "Folklore Translation," "Japanese Film" and "Japanese Business" courses. All 38 US participants were native English speakers between 20 and 23 years old, with the exception of three students who had learned Chinese as a first language at the same time as English.

All of the Japanese students in the experimental ($n = 26$) and comparison ($n = 11$) groups at Tohoku University were first year university students enrolled in the same two English classes ("English Reading" and "English Communication"). The 26 students in the Japanese experimental group volunteered to participate in the Skype activity in addition to their regular classes. All 37 participants were native Japanese speakers between 19 and 20 years old, and were paid to participate in the program.

*1.2.2.2 Procedures*

Before the program started, learners in all four groups completed a preprogram assessment of speaking. Program participants were also given a short survey before the program began that asked about their hobbies, available times, and their area of study at school in order to maximize favorability when matching Japanese and US students. Upon completion of the preassessments, the US and Japanese learners in the experimental groups participated in oral activities via Skype with their partners. These activities were established under the following parameters:

1. During Skype sessions, each pair should communicate in both English and Japanese for at least 15 minutes each, for a total minimum of 30 minutes per session (although they were encouraged to converse longer if they liked).
2. Skype sessions should happen between pairs at least twice per week for a total of 15 continual weeks during the US 2015 spring semester.

Program participants were assigned topics to discuss during one of the two weekly sessions, for example, their hometown, university life, study abroad, a trip they took, and so on. However, so as to provide a minimally restrictive conversational opportunity, students were instructed to begin the conversation about the assigned topic and then expand on it in any way they liked. During the second weekly session, participants engaged in free conversation.

The speaking ability of the US learners at UNC Charlotte was considered to be quite low at the time of enrollment in the program, and thus, they were given in-class scaffolding in the form of activities to help them become able to converse in Japanese smoothly and enjoyably prior to their Skype sessions. For homework, students were required to: (1) write a one-page paper in order to prepare to discuss topics in Japanese, (2) submit the homework assignment to their instructor, and (3) receive back on their paper in the form of instructor proofreading. During the class-hour students orally exchanged topics in pairs based on their revised homework assignments. This activity was conducted one week prior to actual Skype sessions in preparation for talking with their partners, and 20 minutes was used for this activity each class-hour. The remainder of class time was used for activities such as debates and cooking demonstrations. However, as the English learners at Tohoku University were considered higher-level speakers of English and their semester ended in the middle of the US semester (meaning they were not enrolled in any sort of English classes for half of the program), they were not given similar scaffolding.

Data was taken from participants in the form of: (1) pre- and posttests to measure the development of the students' speaking abilities, (2) a one-page reflection paper to examine student perspectives and motivation toward participation in the program, and (3) a questionnaire on their Skype experiences (see Appendix 1.1). This data was analyzed and reported in Kato et al. (2016), and some of the major findings and postanalysis are presented in the next section.

### 1.2.3 Indications of success

"Success" with an educational program can mean different things depending on the program, and a number of factors that help students in different ways must be considered when evaluating one. Many educational programs, such as the Skype partner program, look not only to impart knowledge but also to build skills, provide experiences and interactions, motivate long-term learning, and impact student attitudes. This section will look at the various impacts that the Skype partner program had on participants and analyze its success from a variety of viewpoints.

### 1.2.3.1 Frequency and length of Skype sessions

One of the purposes of the Skype partner program was to provide experiences and interactions for spoken practice. As previously argued, both input and practice are crucial for FL language learners, but chances to practice speaking are especially rare for minor FL learners. To ensure that students were making good use of this opportunity, we first checked the length and frequency of their Skype sessions. Self-reported data taken from our first rendition revealed that a majority (86%) of the participants met or exceeded the 30-minute minimum expectation for conversation length, and a great majority (88%) reported speaking both languages in approximately equal amounts. In addition, a little over two-thirds (67%) of the participants stated that the number of sessions (two sessions per week) provided a reasonable level of practice, and over three-quarters (79%) indicated that the duration of the program (15 weeks) afforded a suitable quantity of input. Thus, it seems that the program was rather successful in providing opportunities and learning experiences to participants.

### 1.2.3.2 Objective measures of speaking

Another purpose of the program was to positively impact learners' oral proficiencies. To examine success in this area, we used objective measures of speaking taken from pre- and posttests, specifically looking at spoken fluency (as measured by speech rate) and complexity (as measured by mean length of utterance).

As reported in Kato et al. (2016), we found that the speech rate of the US participants of Japanese showed a statistically significant increase ($p = 0.005$), whereas that of the US learners in our comparison group did not. Furthermore, a significant interaction was found between participation in the Skype partner program and an increase in speech rate for the US learners of Japanese ($p = 0.017$). Kato et al. (2016) also found that the Japan EFL learners who participated in the Skype partner program exhibited improved speech rates ($p = 0.001$), and much more improvement than non-participants, yielding a significant interaction between participation in the program and improvement ($p = 0.002$). These results indicated that both groups of learners improved their fluency in their respective TLs, due in at least part to their participation in the Skype partner program.

We also checked for differences in spoken complexity between pre- and posttests by looking at participants' mean length of utterance (the average number of words spoken without pausing). The US learners of Japanese, both the comparison group and Skype partner program participants exhibited an increase in their mean length of utterance (Kato et al., 2016). However, participants in the Skype partner program improved more than learners who did not participate, resulting in a significant interaction between participation in the program and improvement in mean length of utterance ($p = 0.007$). Similar results were found for Japanese learners of English who participated in the Skype partner program who improved their mean length of utterances much more than learners who did not participate ($p < 0.001$).

### 1.2.3.3 Students' opinions of the Skype partner program

Another purpose of the Skype partner program was to positively impact student motivation and attitudes toward learning, as this is most important for overcoming the poverty of interest that learners of minor FLs experience. Here, we used student surveys and reflection papers to gauge student opinions to learn how their motivation and attitudes were affected by participation in the program. Data from the reflection papers were analyzed through a conceptually clustered matrix analysis, as per Miles and Huberman (1944).

As reported in Kato et al. (2016), through student surveys we found that participants generally reported that they enjoyed the program (72%), and that at least 70% expressed interest in continuing to talk via Skype with their partner after completion of the program. Not all of the comments were positive, though, and we noted that some of the Japanese participants claimed that they could not find topics to talk about their partner with and one even suggested exchanging partners in the middle of the semester.

We also found that US students who submitted reflection papers were very positive about their experiences in the program. Most (92%) of the 24 students who submitted a paper mentioned within that they enjoyed conversing with their partners, and their comments were overwhelmingly positive. For example, some students wrote that the experience was "amazing" and "important," and one expressed that she wanted to "continue to Skype [with her partner] after [the] program" and maintain her friendship with her partner.

The reflection papers also elucidated some shifts in student attitudes. For example, nearly half of the students mentioned that both their confidence and perceived speaking competencies had improved due to participation. For example, one student commented, "I feel that [the] fluidity of my speech and my readiness to speak in Japanese ... both improved dramatically." Furthermore, many students noted changes in their own attitudes, such as one student who wrote "I became more confident in my language ability in making mistakes ... [before] I was afraid of speaking

Japanese out of embarrassment." Students even found themselves warming up to the idea of the technologies involved, with one student commenting that they were considering not taking the class because of the Skype requirement, but that they were surprised as they "grew to be very comfortable with Skype," which led them to be able to "speak more casually than before." Finally, several participants also mentioned that the program enabled them to experience the Japanese language in its original cultural context, which they felt created better learning experiences.

Although most participants were very positive toward the Skype partner program, several negative comments found in participant reflection papers made us realize that there was still room for improvement. For example, some students lamented the speed with which their partners' spoke their native language. Others found it difficult to schedule appropriate times to talk with their partner because of the 13-hour time gap between the United States and Japan. Finally, some US students were disappointed in the lack of effort from some of their partners, which was likely due to the fact that the Japanese students were participating as volunteers and not receiving course credit, creating an imbalance in partner motivation.

### 1.2.4 Conclusions from the case study

The results given here and detailed in Kato et al. (2016) suggest that VSCMC learning programs can help learners of minor FLs in three major ways: by providing educational experiences and speaking practice opportunities, promoting spoken fluency and complexity, and enhancing motivation and improving attitudes toward learning the TL. These benefits mostly help to tackle the poverty of opportunity problem, as it provides chances to speak with native speakers of their TL, which learners seem to take great advantage of. The fact that students felt more engaged and proactive about their learning indicates that VSCMC can also help to alleviate the poverty of interest problem to some degree. Furthermore, Kato et al. (2016) suggest that VSCMC programs can be mutually beneficial and positive impacts can be made on two groups of students that are learning each other's native language. This is important because one challenge in creating such a program is finding partners for students. However, if the program is designed in such a way that another group of students (such as the English learners in Japan in the case study here) can also benefit, finding partners becomes easier.

### 1.2.5 Advice for creating VSCMC for learners of minor foreign languages

Although this section reported on a program between Japanese and US students who were studying each other's native languages, the same formula can be adapted to other language partnerships. If instructors of minor FLs wish to create VSCMC programs such as the one introduced in this chapter, the results of Kato et al. (2016) and those of a three-year study of our VSCMC program (Spring, Kato, & Mori, 2019) can be very informative, as well as the integrative idea presented in the next section.

First of all, when looking for native speaker partners for students, partner institutions at which students are learning the others' language are highly recommended. This allows for mutually beneficial learning and increases the chances of having active participants, which helps to ensure that interactions are meaningful. This is supported not only by Kato et al. (2016) but also Spring et al. (2019), which looked at the outcomes of data collected from three years of the Skype partner program and makes the same recommendation.

Second, according to the results of Spring et al. (2019), one should not expect to see as much improvement in overall fluency until after students have had four to five semesters, that is, 240–300 hours, of language learning, although the other positive aspects of VSCMC (e.g., increased motivation, interest and meaningful interactions) can still be achieved in lower levels. Low-level students are often intimidated by the idea of communicating with a native speaker partner one on one, so instructors should provide instruction on communicative strategies and scaffolding activities prior to sessions for such students such as premeditated topic selection and specific preparation (e.g., vocabulary, phrases, and pronunciation), related homework assignment for additional preparation, teacher feedback before VSCMC sessions, and in-class practice with other students based on instructor feedback. These exercises are necessary for students up to the intermediate-mid level, but become less critical for higher-level learners, that is, intermediate-high and above. For higher-level learners, I recommend selecting more difficult topics and reducing preparation to written homework assignments. Although lower-level topics can be used for higher-level students, students will likely not require preparation.

Third, VSCMC sessions should not be dominated by either participant. Instructors should strive to ensure that both partners have adequate chances to speak so that they are actually conversing. Although they cannot monitor every interaction, they can teach communication strategies such as giving responses during conversation. This is especially important for lower-level learners of Japanese who might be less proactive due to limited speaking ability. For example, an instructor might teach some simple, but useful phrases in the TL that students can use to respond to their partner in a variety of situations such as "well, let's see," "yes, I think so," "that's surprising!," and "I'm sorry to hear that." Set phrases can help to reduce anxiety and make conversations progress more smoothly.

Finally, making sure that both groups of students are properly incentivized is crucial to the success of the program. For example, in the case study presented here, the Skype partner program could not be offered during the semester for both groups of students because of scheduling differences in Japan and the United States. Consequently, Japanese participants could not receive a grade and did not take the program as seriously, which is not ideal because it creates a motivation gap in partner pairs. However, even if both sets of students cannot receive course credit, other measures can be taken, such as having participants receive credit toward another program, or having participants work collaboratively on a project or problem, as suggested in the next section.

By following this advice and considering integrating project-based language learning into VSCMC programs, as suggested in the next section, instructors of minor FLs can help their students overcome the poverty of opportunity problem and work toward solving the poverty of interest. This is important not only for student improvement, as detailed in this section, but also for prolonged learning and maintaining student interest in general.

## 1.3 Tackling the poverty of interest problem with project-based language learning

Although VSCMC can help FL teachers to solve the poverty of opportunity problem and increase their students' oral proficiencies, there are a number of problems to be addressed when conducting such Internet-based programs, as I discovered in running my own Skype partner program (Kato et al., 2016) and as pointed out by other studies (e.g., Hafner, Li, & Miller, 2015; Taillefer & Munoz-Luna, 2014). One such difficulty is providing students with the appropriate amount of motivation and willingness to communicate (Kato et al., 2016). This section introduces how I made improvements to the Skype partner program in these areas by incorporating project-based language learning and indicates that students' motivation was enhanced as compared to the study outlined in the previous section.

### 1.3.1 Theoretical motivation for implementing PBLL

Project-based learning is a teaching method based on social constructivism (Beckett & Slater, 2005; Dooly & Sadler, 2016; Forester & Meyer, 2015; Vygotzky, 1978). It has been well regarded as a beneficial way for students to learn, as it promotes not only learning of subject matter, but also learner-autonomy and collaborative skills (Beckett & Slater, 2005; Bell, 2010; Forester & Meyer, 2015). In recent years, L2/FL teachers and researchers have implemented project-based learning into their classrooms, creating a new type of approach, which specifically works to improve FL learning. Many studies have been conducted showing that project-based language learning (henceforth, PBLL) can offer numerous benefits such as enhanced social interaction (Beckett & Miller, 2006), facilitated intercultural communication competence (Godwin-Jones, 2013), improved willingness to communicate (Farouck, 2016) and extension of learning over longer periods of time (Warschauer & De Florio-Hansen, 2003). Many researchers have also reported that PBLL brought about improvements specifically related to TL learning. For example, Dooly and Sadler (2016) indicated that their implementation of PBLL allowed students to become immersed in their TL, bolstering their language practice and content knowledge acquisition as a part of the same process. Also, studies such as Ratminingsih (2015), Farouck (2016), Liu (2016) and Maftoon, Birjandi, and Ahmadi (2013) have reported that PBLL can improve L2/FL learners' motivation and willingness to communicate.

Because both VSCMC and PBLL have a number of reported benefits for both L2/FL learning and are both based on social constructivism, aiming to enhance the quality of interactions, these teaching approaches complement each other well and can potentially work in tandem to promote the acquisition of the same types of communicative skills. In reviewing some of the shortcomings of long-distance VSCMC programs, specifically the one outlined in the previous section, that is, loss of interest, nervousness and lack of willingness to communicate, it seems that PBLL could enhance such programs by offering increases and correcting imbalances in motivation, as well as improving the quality of interactions by offering real-world problems for learners to solve cooperatively through project work. In fact, this idea has already begun to be tested in works such as Hafner et al. (2015), who reported positive effects for FL learners when using a combination of PBLL and computer-mediated communication, although the study was not on long-distance VSCMC and did not focus specifically on the outcomes of this program – rather on the use of plurilingualism in the participants' communications.

Based on the negative comments given by students in the 2015 program, as reported in the last section and in Kato et al. (2016), and the potential benefits of PBLL, there was reason to believe that combining PBLL and VCSMC could improve learning conditions in the Skype partner program, and I decided to combine the two by adding a collaborative project into the existing program. However, there were a number of challenges that I faced. For example, the program is long-distance and the participants never actually meet each other. Although Hafner et al. (2015) reported positive learning outcomes for combined PBLL and computer-mediated learning, they reported on students who physically met in class and used computer-mediated learning in addition. Thus, I once again took data with my colleagues to discover the potential limitations and benefits of combining PBLL with our long-distance VSCMC program.

### 1.3.2 A case study of VSCMC-integrated PBLL

In 2017 Skype partner program, the basic settings of the previous program (i.e., length and amount of talking sessions, the classes students were participating in, etc.) did not change from 2015 with the exception of assigning students a project that they needed to complete with their partner.

### 1.3.2.1 Participants

For our 2017 rendition of the Skype partner program, we partnered English language learners at Tohoku University in Japan and Japanese language learners at UNC Charlotte, as in Kato et al. (2016). Twenty-five students participated from each university and were considered our experimental group. Fourteen students at UNC Charlotte and 12 students at Tohoku University participated in our study as a comparison group, taking the same pre- and posttests, but not participating in the program. The basic conditions of the participants were the same as those reported in Kato et al. (2016) in that UNC Charlotte participants were predominantly native English speakers with Japanese ability ranging from elementary-mid to intermediate-mid, and Tohoku University participants being entirely Japanese native speakers with higher English abilities. Furthermore, as in 2015, our program was run according to the UNC Charlotte semester, and thus Tohoku University students could not receive course credit for participating, either, although they could receive points toward a university-wide educational program (the Tohoku Global Leader program[1]).

### 1.3.2.2 Procedures

The same basic procedures were used in our 2017 rendition of the program as per the previous section (Kato et al., 2016). Participants were partnered based on the same short survey taken before the program that asked about their hobbies, majors, and the times they were able to participate in the program. Students were allowed to use any sort of VSCMC device or application, for example, Skype or the Japanese application "Line." Participants were asked to speak in Japanese and in English for at least 15 minutes each per session (for at least two 30-minute sessions each week) for 15 weeks (as per Kato et al., 2016), but in 2017 they were instructed to have one "Topic session," in which they talked about a set topic, and one "PBLL session," in which they were to communicate with the goal of working to complete a project set out at the beginning of the program.

The project for PBLL in 2017 was set as the creation of a homepage (henceforth, HP) that would promote exchange between the two universities and offer helpful information to current and future exchange students. This project was chosen by instructors in advance because the two universities had begun a study abroad exchange agreement in 2015, and the number of exchange students between the two universities had been steadily increasing each year, but there was still not enough information available to prospective students. The topic was selected in order to fulfill the needs of society, a requirement for PBLL projects as per Blumenfeld, Soloway, Marx, Krajcik, Guzdial, and Palinscar (1991), namely, exchange students and the two universities and their foreign student communities. With regard to the information that would be included on the website, the students were asked to select topics that they thought would be beneficial and of interest to study abroad students themselves. The topics included introductions of various restaurants, history of the universities and transportation in the areas. Collaborative activities, which were conducted with partners during the PBLL session, included selecting relevant information, researching topics and related information at both universities, and creating bilingual descriptions. For example, a pair that selected on-campus dining as a topic would discuss which restaurants to report on with their partner, find information, and then write bilingual descriptions for them. Participants would also gather data such as pictures, the menus, and other information on each restaurant and include them in their final project. Participants wrote information for both universities in their TL, and received proofreading and advice from their partners. These were then uploaded using the free website host and creation platform "wix.com." The final product was shared on the homepage and SNS of Tohoku University's Global Learning Center, and is continually presented to UNC Charlotte students who are considering studying abroad in Japan in the future.

It was challenging for UNC Charlotte students whose Japanese language skills were lower than their partners' English to work on the project because the speech acts required to complete a project are more complex than simple discussions. Therefore, scaffolding was provided to help them work on the project with their Skype partners smoothly. In the class-hours of the "Oral Communication" course in the United States, students were required to give an oral progress report once every two weeks for a total of seven times during the semester so that the instructor could monitor students and offer advice as needed. UNC Charlotte students reported their progress in Japanese, including the information they had collected, problems they encountered, and improvements they planned to make in the next phase. Their progress and the appropriateness of their activities was checked through these oral progress reports and the use of a Skype log in which students reported the times, dates, and a summary of what they had spoken about with their partners, as well as any problems or challenges they were facing. Prior to uploading their final product, UNC Charlotte students had to collect the bilingual descriptions and information on their topics for both universities and submit the paper for final proofreading by the instructor. At the end of the semester students gave a presentation, showing their website to their peers. The website was also shared with potential future students who were considering studying abroad at the partner schools through the study abroad offices of both universities. Figures 1.1–1.4 show screenshots of the website.

*Utilizing technology* 25

*Figure 1.1* Title page: "UNCC Tohoku" website.

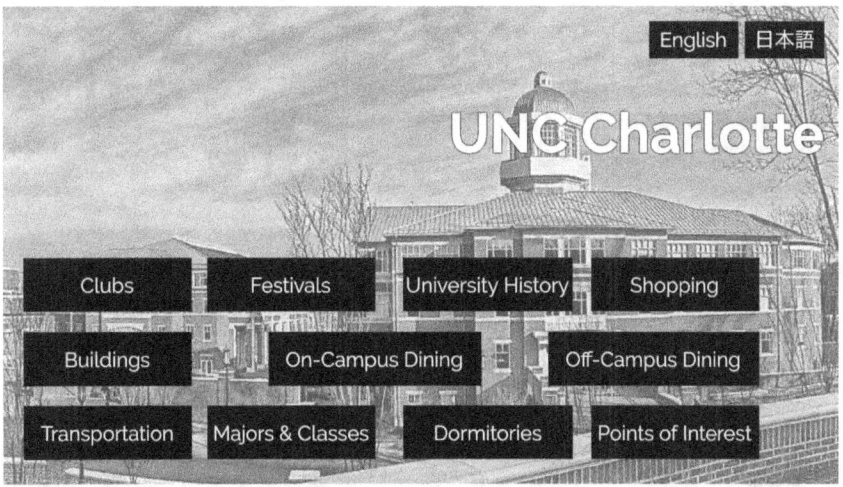

*Figure 1.2* Contents: UNC Charlotte.

### 1.3.3 Indications of success

The same procedures of collecting student data as described in Section 1.2 were used for the 2017 rendition of our program, that is, pre- and posttests of speaking given to experimental and comparison groups and student reflection papers and surveys given only to the Skype partner

26  *Utilizing technology*

*Figure 1.3* Contents: Tohoku University.

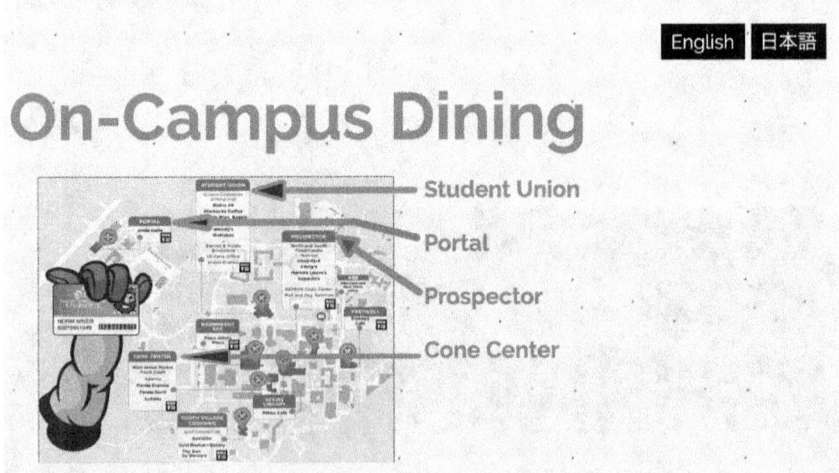

*Figure 1.4* On-campus dining at UNC Charlotte.

program participants. The participants from whom we were able to collect pre- and posttest data in 2017 consisted of 25 US and 10 Japanese experimental group participants, and 12 US and 8 Japanese comparison group participants.

### 1.3.3.1 Frequency and length of Skype sessions

The results of the survey ($N = 35$; 24 US participants, 10 Japanese participants, 1 no answer) revealed that one-half of the students communicated for 30 to 40 minutes, according to program guidelines. Only 2 US students conversed for less than 30 minutes per session, 12 conversed for 40–60 minutes, and 3 reported conversing for more than one hour per session, indicating that most (94%) of the participants met or exceeded the 30 minutes minimum expectation for conversation length. Also, over two-thirds (68%) of the participants spoke their TL in an equitable manner.

### 1.3.3.2 Objective measures of speaking

The US experimental group improved both their speech rates ($p = 0.05$) and mean length of utterance ($p < 0.001$), whereas the US comparison group did not show improvement in their speech rates ($p = 0.59$), but did improve their mean length of utterance ($p = 0.01$). The Japanese experimental group did not improve their speech rate ($p = 0.44$) or mean length of utterance ($p = 0.06$), and neither did the Japanese comparison group (speech rate: $p = 0.41$, mean length of utterance: $p = 0.29$), although this may have been due to the low number of participants who provided speaking data. However, a significant interaction was observed between participation in the program and improvement in mean length of utterance ($p = 0.04$) for Japanese participants, indicating that participants did seem to improve more than the comparison group.

### 1.3.3.3 Comparison of the student responses between 2015 and 2017

In total, 35 (25 US students, 10 Japanese students) out of 50 students in the experimental groups responded to the surveys. In comparing the responses of the same survey questions asked during the program run in 2015 (Kato et al., 2016), it seems that the addition of PBLL in 2017 was successful in improving motivation. Positive student response ratios for the two Likert-style questions, "I enjoyed the program" and "I would like to stay contact with my partner," increased by 13% and 14%, respectively. In the comment column, one-third of the students wrote about their enjoyment saying things such as, "It was interesting for me to touch with native English," and the same number of students noted that they learned many things, noting, "the topics were very helpful in building my vocab and confidence." One-fifth of the students described the program as "the best" method to practice conversation. However, one-fifth of the students pointed out that their partner's attitude was unfavorable, with one student writing, "My partner was usually late; sometimes she would not even show up." One-seventh of the students claimed that it was difficult to get certain info on the region, writing, "My partner knew hardly anything about Sendai[2] because he was not from the area."

In total, 34 students (25 US students, 9 Japanese students) submitted one-page reflection papers in which they wrote freely about the program, and this data was then analyzed through a conceptually clustered matrix analysis (Miles & Huberman, 1944). A great majority of the Japanese students (88%) and over two-thirds of the US students reported satisfaction at having learned various things such as details about their partner, their culture, and much vocabulary. Approximately two-thirds of the Japanese and US students expressed having enjoyed the program, writing, "I really enjoy and treasure every moment that we have. ... The weekly assignment takes time to work on but I love to spent time for it." Over one-half of the US students felt that their language ability had improved, gained confidence in conversing with native Japanese speakers, and claimed to have become better able to understand what their partners were saying in Japanese. Over one-third of both US and Japanese students noted satisfaction with the experience itself, saying, "I could have an experience which generally we cannot have." A little less than one-third of the students intended to continue to converse with their partners after the program, and expressed interest in meeting their partner when they travel to Japan or the United States. One-quarter of the students also expressed positive opinions regarding the project, such as one who commented that it was a "wonderful method to promote the study abroad program."

However, nine US students also wrote about difficulties at the beginning of the semester, such as one who wrote about "how scared [he] was of having to talk to a Japanese student at first." However, as pointed out by Spring et al. (2019), having such difficulties is not necessarily a bad thing, as students who have such challenges and overcome them often make great improvements in oral ability. Another negative opinion given by four US students was that they lost their partners in the latter half of the semester for various reasons, such as Daylight Saving Time, causing scheduling conflicts and Japanese students becoming busy during or after spring vacation. Because of this, there were a few students who could not find a reliable partner.

### 1.3.4 Conclusions from the case study

Based on the results and observations of this study and as reported in Kato et al. (forthcoming), integrating PBLL into long-distance VSCMC programs is possible, and can improve student motivation. This becomes clear when student engagement and opinions of the 2017 program are compared with the 2015 program. Furthermore, the data seems to suggest that adding PBLL to VSCMC does not decrease its effectiveness to improve participant oral communication skills. The participants were found to be interested in the task of developing a HP, and also pointed out several benefits of the PBLL approach, though technical problems can cause frustration (Kato et al., forthcoming). In the case study, students used "wix.com" to create their HP, but it could not be used collaboratively and this was not discovered until the final stages of the project when students started to upload their articles. However, because IT skills and technology in teaching are continually being integrated into society, these skills are important to master, and these problems will hopefully be less prominent in the future.

### 1.3.5 Advice for creating VSCMC combined with PBLL

Based on the case study presented here, I have three pieces of advice for educators looking to integrate PBLL into a VSCMC program.

First, I advise recruiting study abroad students who are native speakers of the students' TL and visiting your institution to help with the program. When Japanese partners in Japan were unavailable for Skype sessions, I allowed students to conduct their tasks with the Japanese study abroad students at our university and record this practice session in their Skype logs. However, this treatment is possible only if you can recruit such study abroad students as supplementary partners at your own institution in advance.

Second, in order to help solve the poverty of interest and balance motivation, we integrated a measure by which Japanese participants could receive some credit for completing the project. Although it was not course credit, it was something that some students wanted, and thus was extrinsically motivating. There will often be times when both groups of students cannot participate for course credit, but finding some sort of credit to offer students who are not participating in the program as part of a class can be very important for balancing motivation amongst partners.

Finally, consider selecting an appropriate project for your students based on their interests and language abilities. Selecting a relevant, inspiring and interesting project enhances and maintains their intrinsic motivation to participate. In the 2017 rendition of our program, instructors decided upon a website project in advance and asked our students to select the topics for the website themselves. For better results, instructors could perhaps suggest a few projects to students, ask them to select their favorite one, or students could suggest other projects themselves through brainstorming. Student motivation could potentially be further increased by allowing them to select the project themselves rather than being assigned one by an instructor. However, remember that the final project should be utilizable and useful in their academic field or their community, either domestically or internationally (Blumenfeld et al., 1991). Future work could test other types of project selections in similar such program to determine what sorts of problems can be solved through the Internet without partners physically meeting.

## Appendix 1.1 Skype partner program survey (questions only)

Name:_____ Your Partner:_____

1. I enjoyed participating in "Let's Talk on Skype Project":
   1. Strongly disagree   2. Disagree   3. Neutral   4. Agree
   5. Strongly agree

2. The Skype Project fulfilled my expectations.
   1. Strongly disagree   2. Disagree   3. Neutral   4. Agree
   5. Strongly agree

3. How long was the *average* session?
   1. Less than 30 minutes      2. 30–45 minutes
   3. 46–60 minutes             4. Over one hour

4. On average, what percentage of the session was conducted in Japanese?
   1. Less than 40%   2. Around 50%   3. Over 60%

5. Would you like to stay in contact with your Skype partner?
   1. No       2. Yes

6. You were required to talk with your Skype partner *twice a week*. How do you feel about the frequencies?
   1. Too much       2. Appropriate       3. More, the better.

7. This project lasted 15 weeks. How do you feel about the length of the project?
   1. Too long       2. Appropriate       3. Too short

8. Please share any additional comments about the "Let's Talk on the Skype Project"

## Notes

1. "The Tohoku Global Leader program" is a certification program at Tohoku University that encourages students to become global citizens.
2. Tohoku University is in the city of Sendai, and so partners had to write about it, but many students at Tohoku University come from other areas of Japan, and first year students often know little about Sendai.

# 2 Educational strategies

## 2.1 Introduction

This chapter describes two educational strategies that can be integrated into minor FL classes to increase intrinsic motivation and facilitate learning outcomes, and how to best implement them. The first section focuses on inter-collaborative peer learning in which TL native speakers and advanced learners registered for the same course to enhance their interpersonal communication abilities, and the second section introduces interventions to enhance learner autonomy in which learners monitor their own learning, self-assess their performance every week and then receive feedback from their instructor. These strategies target the poverty of opportunity and poverty of interest problems by providing chances for learners to get individualized attention from native speakers and their instructors, and by boosting awareness of their own motivation levels.

## 2.2 Tackling poverty of opportunity and interest through inter-collaborative peer learning

Because the poverty of opportunity is one of the most difficult challenges for learners of minor FLs, educators must work to provide learners with as many different chances as possible to speak, listen, and communicate with native speakers in their TL, especially since they are critical for both student motivation and fostering TL competencies (Ellis, 1985; Rubin & Thompson, 1994; Scarcella & Oxford, 1992, Towndrow & Vallance, 2004). One way to provide such opportunities is through inter-collaborative peer learning, such as the Skype partner program, detailed in Chapter 1, which helped students studying Japanese at UNC Charlotte to overcome the poverty of opportunity and poverty of interest via Internet technology. However, although this program was successful in fulfilling its purposes, it was not without its problems.

One problem found in the Skype partner program, was that some partners were not always available at the same times and the learners at UNC Charlotte were often at the mercy of their partner's schedules. In order to alleviate this problem, learners in the program who could not always work with their Skype partners were allowed to work with Japanese study abroad students who were visiting UNC Charlotte. These students worked on their projects in both Japanese and English and used these study sessions in place of Skype sessions. After the 2017 rendition of the program, one student disclosed that communicating with Japanese study abroad students at UNC Charlotte was easier because there was no time difference, making them easier to get in touch with.

Thus, although the Skype partner program was designed to help provide opportunities and raise interest for learners, it did not always have the intended effect, particularly for US learners when their partners were unavailable or inflexible. However, because the idea of mutually beneficial communicative activities seems to be effective at improving oral abilities when it goes well (Kato, Spring, & Mori, 2016; Spring, Kato, & Mori, 2019), a new class was offered to recreate these conditions between US JFL learners and Japanese ESL (English as a second language) learners studying abroad at UNC Charlotte. While this is not a valid option for all minor FL teachers, it can become one if educators work to increase incoming study abroad programs (see Introduction and Chapter 4). Thanks to the increases in the number of incoming Japanese study abroad students at UNC Charlotte, an inter-collaborative course could be created, the first trial of which began in the spring semester of 2019 and was called "Inter-Collaborative Peer Learning." This section gives the theoretical underpinnings of the class, explains how it was implemented, and finally shares preliminary findings that help to underscore the positive benefits to both groups of students.

### 2.2.1 *The theory behind inter-collaborative language learning*

The double immersion teaching approach has been in existence in the United States for half a century, and has recently been increasing throughout the world (Amrein & Peña, 2000; Freeman, 2000; Howard, Sugarman, & Christian, 2003; Kibler, Salerno, & Hardigree, 2014; Wiese, 2004). This approach refers to having peers collaborate to learn each other's first languages, but is referred to by several different names in the wide body of literature, including two-way immersion, double immersion, dual language immersion, bilingual immersion, hybrid language instruction, and two-way bilingual instruction (Wiese, 2004). Howard et al. (2003) reviewed reports conducted by the Center for Research on the Education of Students Placed at Risk, which examines a wide range of topics in early education through high school, and found that though native Spanish speakers in the United States, were increasing, their drop-out rate was extremely high, generally amongst low-income students (Freeman, 2000). They also noted that the United States has had a weak foreign language education system, resulting in few students with familiarity with other languages and cultures. Double immersion programs began to emerge in the United States as a way to solve these problems, providing native English speakers with opportunities to develop foreign language proficiency and second language speakers with chances to study with native English speakers. Amongst the studies examining these dual immersion programs, the learning approach was always with native speakers in the classroom assisting second language learners in gaining vocabulary and syntax, and native speakers benefitting by acquiring metalinguistic awareness through class activities (Howard et al., 2003). Howard et al. (2003) also found that double immersion program participants performed better on standardized achievement tests than their peers and made more progress toward bilingualism, biliteracy and cross-cultural awareness.

Collaborative language learning programs in which language-minority and majority students learn each other's languages together, are most common in elementary schools in the United States between Spanish-dominant English language learners and English-dominant Spanish language learners (Amrein & Peña, 2000; Freeman, 2000; Howard et al., 2003; Kibler et al., 2014) and report varying results. For example, Kibler et al. (2014) designed an extracurricular high school program with ethnolinguistic goals and found that participants of the program developed oral competencies through communicating with their peers, eavesdropping on native speakers' authentic conversations and gained confidence in their TL listening abilities, and exhibited increased communicative competence and ethnolinguistics awareness. However, according to Freeman (2000), who investigated a two-way dual-language program in a middle school designed to challenge language prejudice against L2s and L2 speakers, there were several discrepancies between the idealistic plan and actual implementation. As a wide range of program models exist in the previous studies of bilingual education programs, Wiese (2004) and Amrein and Peña (2000) have suggested that they need to be analyzed on a case-by-case basis, as their success is affected by the design, defined goals and actual implementation.

Other studies have looked at collaborative learning grounded through a sociocultural lens, which emphasizes solving problems and achieving goals cooperatively in linguistically, culturally and academically different groups in order to complete their tasks (Gutiérrez, Baquedano-Lopez, Alvarez, & Chiu, 1999). According to Chaves, Baker, Caves, and Fisher (2006), learning through cooperation and collaboration and joint activities facilitates language learning and development, which is corroborated by studies such as Gutiérrez et al. (1999), who examined Spanish native speaking children and Spanish-English bilingual undergraduates who collaborated with each other in English and Spanish via email to accomplish a multipurposed writing. They found that the participants attained dramatic gains in literacy and bilingual learning and development, leading them to conclude that hybrid literacy practice provides a model of "how meaningful collaboration can be created" (Gutiérrez et al., 1999, p. 92).

These studies indicate that a variety of dual-language programs are effective linguistically, socioculturally and academically, but there are fewer examples of such courses in higher education that are specifically designed to promote two-way dual-language usage. Therefore, there was no model to base a university-level class on, and great lengths were taken to ensure that enough linguistic knowledge would be gained to justify its creation, and that this knowledge would be beneficial enough to both groups of students, that is, US and Japanese students, for each to earn course credit. The next section explains how the course was implemented at UNC Charlotte, and the measures taken to check its success in improving the TL competencies and developing the socioculture and ethnolinguistics awareness of both groups.

### 2.2.2 An example of an inter-collaborative peer learning course at the university level

An inter-collaborative peer learning course was offered at UNC Charlotte within the Japanese program, consisting of native English-speaking US JFL learners and native Japanese speaking Japanese ESL learners. The class was designed to provide scaffolding to all students about how to take both teaching and learning roles so that all participants could enhance their interpersonal communicative abilities in their TLs. Through the scaffolding opportunities to interact with native speakers of their TL twice per week, students aimed to improve their TL oral proficiencies. The teaching environment was highly learner-centered in that the instructor's only role was to arrange and assign activities to the students, and the participants learned from each other through collaborating on tasks in pairs or groups. Because students physically met in the classroom, instructors could assign a wide variety of collaborative activities, including more time-consuming out of class activities in which participants had more chances to interact naturally, which was a limitation of the Skype partner program.

While the course described earlier is obviously beneficial for the minor FL learners who are experiencing a poverty of opportunity, there were some concerns with its creation as well. For example, it was not clear if the study abroad students, who are immersed in their TL on a daily basis, would benefit from helping the JFL learners. Another had to do with the requirements of teachers to generate enough interest to have large enough classes that their programs are justified, and this was especially difficult for this course, because it was designed with in-class pair and group work activities in mind, meaning that relatively equal numbers of US JFL and Japanese ESL learners were required, following Kibler et al. (2014). Therefore, it was also unclear if enough Japanese ESL learners would participate in the course.

### 2.2.2.1 Participants

Eligibility guidelines were created for participants: US JFL learners who had completed at least six semesters of Japanese language courses and Japanese study abroad students visiting UNC Charlotte throughout the spring semester of 2019. In total, five US JFL learners (all male; aged 22–29) and six Japanese ESL learners (one male and five females; aged 20–21) registered for the course. All US JFL learners were native English speakers and all Japanese ESL learners were native Japanese speakers.

The English abilities of the Japanese ESL students were higher than the Japanese abilities of the US JFL students, due largely to a difference in the amount of time having spent studying their respective TLs. The Japanese students having learned English for at least six years in middle and high school with further study at their home universities and having met minimum TOEFL score requirements for enrollment at UNC Charlotte. In contrast, US JFL learners had only learned Japanese for three to four years, and their oral abilities in Japanese were considered to be from elementary-high to advanced-low level, as judged through the Oral Proficiency Interview made by the American Council on the Teaching of Foreign Languages (ACTFL). Specifically, of the US JFL students, one was rated to be elementary-high, one intermediate-low, one intermediate-mid, one intermediate-high and one advanced-low (a heritage student). Four of the Japanese study abroad students' oral abilities in English were considered to be intermediate-high, one was advanced-low and one was advanced-mid level.

### 2.2.2.2 Course content

In the first class, the instructor explained the syllabus, course content, and what was expected of students throughout the semester. Students were also encouraged to speak in their TLs as much as possible during the class-hours. Four kinds of class activities were integrated during the class-hours: collaborative project work in pairs, a speaking activity ("Let's talk") in pairs, a topic talk task ("My favorite news") in pairs, and a debate activity in groups. Pair work was selected because it provides learners with "an improved quantity and quality" of L2/FL (Storch & Aldosali, 2012, p. 32). Furthermore, when students interact and communicate with each other, with less involvement from the instructor, they are more comfortable being corrected, and peer error correction is surmised to increase student motivation and reduce monotony more than instructor correction (Achmad & Yusuf, 2014). Because the goals of this class were to enhance oral abilities and provide opportunities to communicate with native speakers, three kinds of pair-work tasks (the collaborative project, "Let's Talk" and "My Favorite News" activities) conducted with one JFL and one ESL learner were set as the primary pair-work class

36  Educational strategies

*Table 2.1* Class schedule in inter-collaborative peer learning course in spring 2019

| Spring 2019 | Activities on Tuesday | Activities on Thursday |
| --- | --- | --- |
| Former half | "Let's talk," debate | Collaborative project, debate |
| Latter half | "Let's talk," debate | "My favorite news," debate |

*Table 2.2* The schedule of the collaborative project in the former half of the semester

| Week | Content |
| --- | --- |
| 1st | Matched a partner, conversed and exchanged their best memories orally |
| 2nd | Wrote down their partners' memory in a script format |
| 3rd | Proofread their partners' script |
| 4th | Created a PowerPoint with use of photos and scripts they had written |
| 5th | Practiced for their presentation |
| 6th | Presentations |

activities. Furthermore, classroom debates were also used as a group work assignment because they have been found to also be effective at enhancing FL processing because students must insist on their own opinions and refute others based on materials prepared in advance, and because they increase opportunities for utterance, and force learners to conduct interact and cooperate as a team (Al-Mahrooqi & Tabakow, 2015; Kato, 2018a; Zare & Othman, 2013).

Table 2.1 shows the class schedule for the spring semester of 2019. Debate activity was conducted throughout the semester, but "Let's talk" was conducted on Tuesday in the former and latter half of the semester, and the collaborative project was conducted on Thursday in former half of the semester with the "My favorite news" activity in the latter. Each class-hour was divided evenly amongst the two class activities shown in Table 2.1.

Table 2.2 shows the schedule of the collaborative project. The collaborative project tasked learners with gathering information from their partner related to a topic that was chosen in advance by the instructor – in this case to find out what their partner's fondest memory is. Students had to not only ask their partner about this topic, but also recreate the story and give a PowerPoint presentation to the class at the end of the former half of the semester. In the sixth class-hour, students gave presentations using their TLs for 10 minutes each, including a question and answer session.

For the "Let's talk" activity, the instructor selected easy topics in advance for the first half of the semester, for example, telling about their favorite movies and their best travel memories, and more difficult topics to develop socioculture awareness such as global warming, gun control in the United States, and the declining birthrate in Japan, in the second half of the semester. In preparation for this activity, students were required to first write one page about the topic in their TL for homework. These writings were submitted to the instructor who then asked native speakers in the class to proofread and correct the assignments and then resubmit them to the instructor, who then returned them to the original authors. In the first class-hour, one JFL learner and one ESL student who proofread the partner's script sat together and the ESL student played the role of instructor, explaining why the JFL learner's mistakes were incorrect. After this teaching and learning session based on the JFL learners' homework assignments, they practiced talking about the topic for about 10 minutes, not only based on what the JFL learners had written in their papers but also beyond this scope. The ESL learners were not given any preparation. Then the instructor asked all of the students to change partners twice after talking for 7–8 minutes each time. This allowed every student to talk about the topic three times with several different partners. JFL learners were not allowed to read their scripts and had to try to talk about the topic without the aid of their prepared statements. The following week, the roles of the JFL and ESL learners were swapped and US students played the instructor role to help teach Japanese students. During this week, ESL learners wrote scripts, and US students checked their English and helped them understand why their mistakes were incorrect. In total, nine "Let's talk" sessions with nine different topics were held during the semester.

The "My favorite news" activity involved students selecting a news article that could be reported to the class in approximately three minutes. Students were asked to select an article, read it in advance, and bring it to class. JFL learners selected one news article from the website "NHK Web Easy," which has a variety of Japanese news articles written in easy Japanese without any English translation. ESL learners could select any English language news article. In the class-hour, JFL and ESL learners reported their selected news articles orally in pairs. After ten minutes, partners were changed, and this was repeated twice so that each student explained their news article to three different partners. Students were asked to focus on speaking smoothly while reporting, looking at the article as little as possible. Five to six students were then required to report their news to the class after finishing the partnered sessions. Each student had to report to the class a total of four times in the latter half of the semester, but they did not know in advance who would be selected to report each time (it was decided by drawing straws) in order to ensure that students were taking the task seriously each time.

The debate activity was conducted in groups to promote collaborative learning and teamwork because students working in small groups develop not only a deeper understanding of the subject matter but also develop key professional competencies such as critical thinking, communication skills, interpersonal relations, self-assessment (Chaves et al., 2006; Qureshi & Stormyhr, 2012). Actual debates were held a total of four times during the semester. In the interest of fairness, groups were formed with an (almost) even number of JFL and ESL learners, and the side that each had to argue for was decided by drawing straws. The groups were changed after each debate. One leader was selected for each group, who was then tasked with stating their groups' strongest opinion first in the actual debate, making a list of difficult vocabulary words, and showing the list to the other group on the day of the debate, which ensured that everyone in the class would have an equal understanding of the subject matter. At the outset of the actual debate, one of the two leaders stated their groups' strongest opinion and then one member of the opposing group stated their opinion in response. All of the students were required to state their opinions in their TLs at least three times during each debate, and leaders were responsible for helping to ensure that each member of their group had at least three opportunities to speak. Students were given five preparation sessions for each debate, as represented in Table 2.3.

Students were required to write all of the opinions (their own, opposing opinions and counterarguments) for the first four sessions, and they were required to submit them after each debate. Specifically, US JFL learners were required to write the opinions using Kanji characters as much as possible. The notes were graded by the instructor based on effort (the number of sentences written in their notes). The debate topics required careful consideration because though debates can be enjoyable and comfortable, they can also become overly difficult and emotionally charged or draining if the topics are highly controversial. Also, if the pros and cons of the debate topic are clearly defined by a majority of people, or most people agree with one side of the issue, it is inappropriate, as this limits the amount of critical thinking that will be involved. As reducing anxiety is important for increasing and maintaining intrinsic motivation in FL/L2 language learning, the first debate topic was set to "Are pets necessary in your life?" The subsequential debate topics were then selected by students to reduce the amount of anxiety from the topics themselves. They chose: Are

*Table 2.3* The schedule of the five sessions for debate activity

| Sessions | Activities |
| --- | --- |
| 1st | Explored and collected opinions for their own side |
| 2nd | Explored and collected opposing opinions |
| 3rd | Wrote counterarguments to opposing opinions |
| 4th | Expanded upon the original opinions and counterarguments |
| 5th | Held mock debates within their groups in preparation for the main debate |

## Educational strategies 39

smartphones necessary for kids? Which is more precious, love or money? Are school uniforms necessary?

### 2.2.3 Indications of success

#### 2.2.3.1 Objective measures of speaking

Because one of the goals of the inter-collaborative peer learning course was to enhance the TL oral proficiency of both groups, data was collected to check for change in speaking ability. As with other verification experiments reported in this book, students were given oral pre- and posttests that were then analyzed through objective measures of speaking, specifically their speech rates as measured in words spoken per minute. All of the Japanese ($n = 6$) and US ($n = 5$) students registered for the course took both tests at the beginning and the end of the semester, but due to technical problems with the recordings, data could only be secured for four ESL and four JFL learners. Unfortunately, statistical analysis was not possible with such a small sample size, but the results were promising for an initial observation. Specifically, the speech rates of all US JFL students slightly increased from their pre- to posttest (+0.63, +0.15, +0.12, +0.09), but only one Japanese ESL student increased upon this same measurement (+0.66, −0.03, −0.37, −0.38). With the current sample size, it is impossible to tell exactly why the ESL students exhibited less improvement than their JFL counterparts, but one reason could simply be statistical noise in the sampling. Another could be that the ESL students had higher proficiencies to start with and ample opportunities to speak their TL outside of the class, so the impact of the class might not have been as large on them as it was on the JFL students, who have fewer opportunities to speak their TL and lower starting levels. However, repeating the same class and getting more data is necessary before making any hard conclusions on this matter.

#### 2.2.3.2 Students' opinions of the inter-collaborative peer learning course (questionnaires and reflection papers)

The other goal of this course was to increase student motivation toward learning and speaking their TLs. Questionnaires and reflection papers were employed to determine the effects of the course in these areas. Questionnaires were conducted anonymously within the class-hour on the last day of the semester (see Appendix 2.1), but two US JFL students were absent and could not respond to the questionnaire ($N = 9$). Summatively, the findings suggest that not only did students enjoy the activities, they did so because of the language practice and awareness that it granted them. Importantly, studies such as Spring et al. (2019) and Nakamura and Spring (forthcoming) point out that while enjoyment alone isn't enough to indicate improvement FL learners who report enjoying activities because of the learning opportunities or linguistic awareness it affords them tend to show improvement (as opposed to those who report no enjoyment or enjoyment for reasons unrelated to education such as comfort or ease).

The results of the questionnaire indicated that all of the students strongly agreed or agreed (on a 5-point Likert scale) with the idea that they enjoyed participating in the course (94%). This is a significant improvement ($\chi^2$ (2, $N$ = 86) = 24.4, $p$ < 00000.1) over the reported enjoyment by participants in the Skype-partner program in 2015 (72%) and 2017 (85%) (see Section 1.3.3 in Chapter 1), indicating that inter-collaborative peer learning in person may be more enjoyable than via the Internet. In the free response section, they indicated the reasons why they enjoyed it, such as that they could make friends (44%), and that it was either a fun or comfortable way to have opportunities to speak in their TL (33%). Actually, all students except two Japanese students (whose English proficiency was advanced level) responded that they had more opportunities to speak English in this class than in any of their other courses taken in the same semester. The participants' responses regarding what they saw as the beneficial points of the pair-work showed that they felt it helped them to improve their TL skills (78%), exchange information about their cultures (i.e., develop socioculture awareness), and learn and teach their target and native languages (67%). Over one-half of the students (55%) found that the course was designed in a way that made it easy to get along with their partners, and learn their TL in several ways. Furthermore, several students (44%) suggested that repeating the same activity with different partners was excellent practice for improving their TL skills. The activities that students selected as their favorites were the two pair-work activities, that is, "Let's talk" (78%) and "My favorite news" (67%), because they found pair-work to be the most effective method to enhance their TL learning. Furthermore, over two-thirds of the students (68%) answered that the homework assignment in preparation for the "Let's talk" activity was effective in increasing their writing ability.

However, some students did point out difficulties with the collaborative project, specifically, that meeting outside of the class-hours was problematic (33%), and the fact that their partner's TL proficiency was much higher than their own caused an imbalance in practice (22%; stated by one US and one Japanese student). Finally, the majority (89%) of the students said that the difficulty level of the class content was too easy, with over one-half of students (55%) responding that they did not face any problems during the class. Although some did report that they had problems (44%), these students did all mention that they could eventually overcome them, which is also associated with improvement in oral proficiency (Spring et al., 2019).

Students were required to write a free-response one-page reflection paper in their L1s about their experiences in the class at the end of the semester, and all participants submitted the assignment ($N$ = 11). Data from the reflection papers were analyzed through a conceptually clustered matrix analysis, as per Miles and Huberman (1944). The students were generally positive in their reflection papers and wrote comments that were largely in line with the responses to the questionnaire. For example, all students (100%) in the class wrote at least one comment about how excited they were to have participated in the class. Representative responses of their overall impression of the class include, "[this was an] enjoyable and valuable class for me in my efforts to gain proficiency in the Japanese language. ... [I] will always treasure the experience" (by a US student), "[this is] the first bilingual class I have ever taken ... [it was] truly a breath of fresh air ... and I looked forward to going to it every Tuesday and Thursday" (by a US student), "[I was] really honored to have learned in a challenging environment" (by a Japanese student), and "[I] could make the best memory in my study abroad experience" (by a Japanese student). Two-thirds of the students felt the dual-immersion was a beneficial method to develop their ethnolinguistic awareness, writing, "hav[ing] a Japanese student check or correct your Japanese and check their [English] is [a] valuable experience" (by a US student), "It was very useful because there weren't many environments where you could hear the subtle difference in [nuance] directly or talk repeatedly about the corrected content" (by a Japanese student). The outcomes of the questionnaire suggested that approximately half of the students felt that one advantage to the class was that they were able to make friends through it, and this notion was supported by the reflection papers in which students gave comments such as, "most importantly, I was able to make a lot of new friends through taking this course. ... These are relationships I hope to maintain and continue to nurture in my life going forward" (by a US student), and "I was able to talk to Americans I met in this class like good friends in Japan" (by a Japanese student). The responses in the reflection papers also corroborated the survey results in that one-third of the students wrote that they felt the pair-work activities, that is, the "Let's talk" and "My favorite news" activities were effective to enhance TL learning. Students noted the merit of communicating with native speakers of their TL, with two US students writing that they felt their Japanese proficiency had improved, and two Japanese students who were struggling to acclimate to US society writing that participating in the course helped them adjust to life there. The remaining two Japanese students indicated that they were glad to communicate with US students who understand Japanese culture and language and that they could develop socioculture awareness through exchanging their cultures and their life styles.

## 2.2.4 Conclusions from the example study

Creating a collaborative class with US students and study abroad students who were native speakers of their TL with the aim of mutually beneficial TL

42  Educational strategies

improvement is still rare in higher education. The initial results of the pilot study presented above suggest that the inter-collaborative peer learning course was successful at providing dual immersion for both the US JFL and the Japanese ESL students to mitigate both the poverty of opportunity and poverty of interest problems. For example, US JFL learners gave comments such as "[this was] the first bilingual class I have ever taken," which indicates that opportunities were indeed being created, and "[it was an] enjoyable and valuable class … will always treasure the experience," which illustrates how the poverty of interest was lessened through the course. It also helped some Japanese ESL students who had trouble integrating into US life before the course to overcome their own poverty of opportunity problems, who said things such as "[this was] the best memory in my study abroad experience." Furthermore, it helped many of the students avoid the poverty of interest problem, as indicated by the responses in the questionnaire and reflection papers in which students claimed that the class was a good experience that helped them develop bonds that they wanted to cherish and maintain, for example, "These are relationships I hope to maintain and continue to nurture in my life going forward" by a US student and "I was able to talk to Americans I met in this class like good friends in Japan" by a Japanese student. Students also spent time together both inside and outside of the class, and made friends, which helped to alleviate both poverty of opportunity and interest, with one student even reporting that all of the students had lunch together after the last class. Although there was concern that the Japanese ESL students would not feel that the course was as useful as their counterparts, their responses to the questionnaire and reflection papers did not support this idea. Rather, the majority of both groups of students found the class and collaborative activities in it beneficial and enjoyable.

With regard to improvement in oral proficiency, this sample size of this study was too small to run any statistical tests, but the qualitative analysis presented earlier are suggestive of a class that was meaningful for improving spoken TL proficiency as well. The initial results reported here are quite promising for the US JFL students, but not as much so for the Japanese ESL students. Some Japanese ESL students mentioned that they felt the class activities were too easy, and this could be the reason that more improvement was not seen in their oral fluency. This is perhaps one primary issue that could be improved in the future. However, it is still unclear how best to tackle this problem, as making the tasks overly difficult for the lower-level US JFL students could cause nervousness and anxiety, which are often associated with deteriorated learning (e.g., Aguila & Harajanto, 2016; Kato, 2007).

### 2.2.5  *Advice for offering inter-collaborative peer learning courses*

When teaching a minor FL, mitigating the poverty of opportunity and poverty of interest problems are of the utmost importance and may be at the forefront of many educators' minds. While there are many ways to do this, this section suggests that utilizing inter-collaborative peer learning can be effective here, while also helping students to improve their TL proficiencies. However, in trying to create such courses or programs, there are a number of considerations of which teachers should be aware.

First of all, a dual immersion course such as the one described in this section may only be available if your institution accepts a number of inbound students from overseas, especially ones that are native speakers of the minor FL that you teach. However, as noted in the Introduction, even if there are not enough study abroad students for you to create a course, a similar program may be feasible if there are short-term visitors or native speakers in the surrounding community. Once you have secured native speakers, there are still a number of other considerations when creating a dual immersion course or program.

In order to create a truly immersive environment for both groups of learners, the number of speakers of both languages should, ideally, be about the same. When conducting pair work such as the activities described in the previous sections, students must both practice their TL and teach their L1. In these situations, one on one communication is best, as it offers evenly balanced benefits to both parties. While it is still possible to create such courses or programs with unbalanced numbers, this may cause disequilibrium in learning outcomes, which might be unfair to one group of learners.

Next, when the proficiency levels of the groups of students are unequal, instructors must take great care to control the difficulty of the activities for each group of students. For example, in the case study presented in this section, the ESL learners had much higher TL ability than the JFL learners. The course reported on in this study might have been too focused on the JFL students, as a few ESL students complained that the course was too easy, so one improvement that could be made over the current configuration is to create activities that are related, but more advanced for the higher-level students. Although it is ideal to balance the levels of the learners as much as possible, it is not always possible. However, future iterations of the course described in the case study could add a prerequisite Japanese ability level so that it would be possible to use more advanced learning materials with all students.

Finally, dual immersion courses or programs should be designed to allow for students to spend as much time as possible practicing speaking through pair work activities. As indicated by the reflection papers and questionnaire reported in this chapter, students felt that these tasks were the most beneficial, and they also seemed to enjoy them the most. In the case study, students conversed for 7–10 minutes per pair, but some students mentioned that it was too short and would have liked to spend more time with one partner. Thus, interpersonal, one-on-one speaking should likely take the main focus of such dual immersion learning.

## 2.3 Interventions to enhance learner autonomy and motivation

Self-assessment is an important skill for learners and providing feedback is an effective tool to enhance student learning. By providing students with the tools to monitor themselves and appropriate feedback, instructors can encourage and facilitate the learning process, promote student motivation levels and reduce attrition rates in language classes. This section introduces intervention strategies for learners of minor FLs and explains the specific benefits of them.

### 2.3.1 The theory behind student interventions: Studies on self-assessment and receiving feedback

In recent years, there has been a major shift in learning assessment from being completely teacher-oriented to more student-generated, this is, self-evaluation (e.g., Tohsaku, 2007). Moritz (1996) regards self-assessment in FL education as a nontraditional form of assessment that is a logical component of both a learner-centered pedagogy and more self-directed (autonomous) learning programs. Self-assessment, one method of self-evaluation, originated in the context of autonomous learning (Blue, 1994), and its procedures are recognized as an effective tool for assisting learners and being a key learning strategy for autonomous language learning (Harris, 1997; Todd, 2002; Tohsaku, 2007; Yang, 1998). Self-monitoring and self-assessment of student progress has become an essential element in language learning as it raises the level of individual linguistic awareness and ultimately promotes learner autonomy, and their usefulness has been widely accepted by many researchers (e.g., Harris, 1997; Todd, 2002; Tohsaku, 2007; Yang, 1998), with Todd (2002) calling self-assessment "a prerequisite for a self-directed learner" (p. 17). This is exemplified by Yang (1998), who integrated activities into ESL classes and reported that these activities were helpful in the promotion of learner autonomy. Self-assessment can also help to make learners more active (Harris, 1997) and increase motivation and enhance learning (Todd, 2002). Promoting learner autonomy also corresponds with maintaining student motivation, which in turn helps with the poverty of interest problem that minor FL learners often face in the long term.

However, self-assessment alone isn't enough to promote learning, as instructor feedback also plays an important role in helping students learn. Specifically, formative feedback has been noted to be a crucial component of the teaching and learning process (Rodgers, Horvath, Jung, Fry, & Diefes-Dux, 2015). A number of studies also suggest that progressive feedback, in combination with self-assessment practices, have even greater effects on academic achievement than either used in isolation (Laurillard, 1993; Lynch & Maclean, 2003; Hyland, 2001; Schunk

& Swartz, 1993). For example, Schunk and Swartz (1993) reported that learners who were instructed to monitor and self-assess their progress and were also provided with instructor feedback performed significantly better compared to learners who did not receive feedback. Furthermore, studies such as Hyland (2001) and Lynch and Maclean (2003) underscore the importance of feedback in the process of language learning, claiming it supports and motivates students. This notion is also suggested by Laurillard (1993) who says that "action without feedback is completely unproductive for a learner" (p. 61), and that integrating self-monitoring, self-assessment and instructor feedback enhance self-confidence.

Based on these studies, student interventions that incorporate both self-assessment and instructor feedback can potentially be effective in assisting, encouraging and motivating learners. Although such procedures can be used in the teaching of any FL, it is particularly useful for learners of minor FLs, who usually have lower motivation rates due to poverty of interest and opportunity. The "Self-Assessment Project" was thus created for use in the Japanese program at UNC Charlotte in 2005, and learner opinions toward the intervention procedures were examined to discover how beneficial the students found it and if there were differences in the preferences among course levels, that is, elementary, intermediate and upper-intermediate classes.

### 2.3.2 An example of a self-assessment project at UNC Charlotte

#### 2.3.2.1 Design and procedure

A Self-Assessment List (see Appendix 2.2) was integrated into all UNC Charlotte Japanese language courses in 2005. It was designed to have students focus on three main intervention elements that would facilitate their learning by:

1. reflecting on their learning processes every week and assessing their learning performance
2. writing journals, questions, problems and any comments they had
3. receiving prompt feedback from their instructors

Students were required to remember what Japanese language skills they had learned in the previous week and write a summary of their accomplishments that week. Students then evaluated their performance the previous week as follows: (1) students assessed their learning using one of three symbols (a ☺ for "Well done," a ∆ for "So-so," and X for "No comment"), and (2) students updated their journals by writing self-assessment comments about their progress.

After inputting the information into their Self-Assessment List forms, students submitted the lists to their instructors, who then reviewed the individual lists and gave written feedback. Prior to the beginning of the semester, all instructors involved in this project read "Directions for scaffolding (making suggestions)" (Rubin, 2003) for providing students with feedback and followed these guidelines. The instructors looked at each column (self-assessment, journals/comments) in the Self-Assessment List and tried to scaffold students' learning of Japanese through the following types of comments:

- encouragement, for example, "You are satisfied with your study. Great!!"
- suggestions, for example, "Come to see me after class"
- reinforcement, for example, "Your Japanese handwriting is so beautiful"
- responses to questions students wrote, for example, "Recall the –te form song"
- questions, "Do you know the –te form song?" or "Were you sick last week?"

Students in each class received a hard copy of the Self-Assessment List and the instructions on the procedures in the first class of the semester, including the purpose of the project and how to fill it out. As Harris (1997) notes, "To be effective, self-assessment must be practical in terms of time and equipment, and must fit into the busy schedule of language classrooms" (p. 18). Therefore, the Self-Assessment List was designed so that students could fill it out in approximately five minutes at the beginning of each class period. Students began evaluating their previous week's learning experiences and accomplishments from the second week of the semester. The lists were returned to the students with instructor feedback the next class period. This activity was integrated into class periods every Monday throughout the semester.

### 2.3.2.2 Participants

All learners of Japanese at UNC Charlotte in the 2005 academic year participated in the self-assessment project and a study held during the fall semester of 2005 helped to evaluate its effectiveness. The L1 of the participating students was predominantly English, with a few exceptions including students whose L1 was Korean, Vietnamese, Taiwanese, and mainland Mandarin Chinese. Over the 2005 academic year, the Japanese program offered two semesters of classes for each of the three levels: elementary, intermediate and upper intermediate. All classes consisted of 4.5 face-to-face teaching hours for three days per week. Student ages ranged from 18 to 35 ($M = 20$), with the majority of the participants being between 18 and 25 years old. Four instructors of Japanese, including the author, were involved in this intervention study. In total, this resulted in 151 student participants (male – 76%, female – 24%) including 97 students in level 1 (elementary I and II), 34 students in level 2 (intermediate I and II) and 20 students in Level 3 (upper-intermediate I and II).

*2.3.2.3 Outcomes of the self-assessment project*

A questionnaire (see Appendix 2.3) was developed in order to evaluate the usefulness of the Self-Assessment List (Kato, 2009). Overall, 106 of the 151 participants submitted the questionnaire. More than half of the students responded positively to all of the seven question items regarding how favorably they viewed the self-assessment project. Specifically, 70% agreed to the three question items regarding whether or not it was: (1) helpful for reviewing learning, (2) useful in assessing achievement, and (3) good for receiving instructor feedback (Kato, 2009).

Student opinions were also checked across levels, that is, elementary, intermediate and upper-intermediate levels, for significant differences. As reported in Kato (2009), both elementary- and intermediate-level students seemed to have similar opinions, with a majority (80%) of lower-level students recognizing the self-assessment project as effective, helpful for monitoring their progress and a positive way to make them think about what they needed to do. They responded to open-ended questions positively, saying, "Self-assessment was a good way to determine learning styles that promote better learning of foreign languages," and "[it was] an effective way of improving [my] Japanese language skills." The great majority (89%) of the elementary-level learners also found the feedback function beneficial and appreciated receiving it, noting that "it really helps to receive feedback from the instructor," which is congruent with the results of other studies that report on similar self-assessment programs (e.g., Hyland, 2001; Lynch & Maclean, 2003).

However, upper-level students' opinions differed significantly ($p < 0.1$) from those of the lower-level students (Kato, 2009). Upper-level students seemed to feel that the activities were troublesome and a waste of time more than the lower-level learners and did not recommend continuing the program, which was contrary to the reactions of the lower-level learners. Some higher-level students left negative comments about the project in the questionnaire, but they did not provide sufficient information to reveal why they did not view the projects as worthwhile. However, there were a couple of noteworthy comments from these students, such as, "I think if you are in college, then you should be able to manage your own study habits without *self-assessment*," and "It was not helpful to me because I sometimes forgot and lost the paper." The fact that higher-level learners

48  *Educational strategies*

did not find the self-assessment program as helpful is in line with other similar studies such as Gabb (2001), which also found that only beginner-level learners found such interventions favorable.

### 2.3.3  Conclusions from the example study

The majority of elementary- and intermediate-level learners in this study agreed that reviewing and self-assessing their performance and receiving feedback from their instructors each week was helpful because it was the first time for them to learn a new foreign language or because they had just begun learning it. They appreciated having close contact with their instructor and utilizing the Self-Assessment List. However, the higher-level learners did not, possibly because they had already overcome their problems in learning Japanese over their previous three or four semesters of study, and may have already understood how to manage their own Japanese learning. Furthermore, only more motivated learners tend to reach higher levels, so it is possible that they were simply already highly motivated and thus did not require help in the form of a self-evaluation or intervention. However, more research is needed to know exactly why this difference of opinions between higher and lower level students was found.

### 2.3.4  Advice for introducing interventions

Although the case study focused on Japanese learners at UNC Charlotte, similar intervention strategies and self-assessment programs can be created for any language learner. However, such intervention strategies are especially important for learners of minor FLs because they often require the most motivation in order to overcome the poverty of interest problem over long periods of time, especially lower-level students. A combined self-assessment and instructor feedback program, such as the one described in the previous sections, is highly recommended for beginning learners of minor FLs, who are more prone to quit studying and withdraw from classes. Helping such students through interventions such as these can reduce their attrition rates and enhance their motivation. However, as suggested by the data from the last section, these strategies are not recommended for students who have been studying their TLs for over three or four semesters.

Technology can also be utilized to lessen the load of self-assessment interventions described in this section. When this strategy was integrated in 2005, a paper list was utilized, but online devices that are far more convenient for both students and instructors are now available. This can be accomplished through LMS (learning management systems) or simple online questionnaire and data collection tools such as Google Forms. Through use of CANVAS, the LMS available at UNC Charlotte, the Japanese program was able to reduce problems that were brought up in the 2005 study, such as losing the self-assessment paper, in future renditions of the program. I also recommend arranging for students to submit a list of their assessment/comments and receive instructor feedback online twice per week. This rate will maximize student benefits from the program, and should not cause too much burden for students or teachers if done online.

Finally, if creating such a self-assessment program, due diligence should be given to the creation of the form. For example, if instructors add the assignments and lesson plans (current lesson number, quizzes, tests, events, etc.) into the form in advance, students can clearly see what assignments will be coming in the future, which ones they missed (if absent), and what they will study each week. This will help them to understand what is expected of them, organize themselves, manage their time, and keep track of the class in general. If the form is made in a way that is useful to them in these ways, the likelihood of them using it and feeling positive toward will likely increase.

## Appendix 2.1 Inter-collaborative project questionnaire

The information provided will in NO way influence your examination results.

Please circle the number(s) of your appropriate response(s).

1   Overall, I enjoyed participating in "Inter-Collaborative Project" course.
    1. Strongly *disagree*   2. Disagree   3. Neutral   4. Agree
    5. Strongly *agree*

    Please write a reason(s) why you selected the above.

    _____

    _____

2   What do you find the *difficult* points in conducting a collaborative project during the former semester? (multiple choice)
    1. Difficult to get along with my partner
    2. Partner's communication ability is poor
    3. Our preference/idea is different
    4. Difficult to find times outside the class-hours
    5 Abilities of my partner's English is super
    6. Did not speak Japanese so often

    Others: Please specify (                                                    )

3. What do you find the *beneficial* points in pair-work conducted in the class-hour? (multiple choice)
   1. Easy to get along with my partner
   2. Could learn Japanese language in several ways
   3. Could repeat my topic a few times
   4. Could improve my Japanese abilities
   5. Could exchange info on our culture
   6. Could learn Japanese and teach English

   Others: Please specify (                                      )

4. What activity(ies) do you think you could increase your Japanese oral ability? (multiple choice)
   1. Collaborative project   2. Debate activity   3. Let's talk
   4. My favorite topic

5. What activity(ies) are your favorite one(s)? (multiple choice)
   1. Collaborative project   2. Debate activity   3. Let's talk
   4. My favorite topic

6. Writing assignment for "Let's Talk" activity helped me to increase my Japanese writing ability.
   1. Yes, I think so   2. Either yes or no   3. No, I don't think so.

7. Is a level of your confidence in speaking Japanese language improved?
   1. Strongly *disagree*   2. Disagree   3. Neutral   4. Agree
   5. Strongly *agree*

8. What do you think of the difficulty of the activities conducted in the class-hour?
   1. Very *difficult*   2. Difficult   3. Just good   4. Easy
   5. Very *easy*

9. I had the most opportunities to speak in Japanese in this class among other Japanese classes taken in this semester.
   1. Strongly *disagree*   2. Disagree   3. Neutral   4. Agree
   5. Strongly *agree*

10. Could you overcome some problems when you faced some difficulties?
    1. No, I couldn't.   2. I didn't face any problems
    3. Yes, I could overcome.

    Please write your comments/suggestions on this course freely if you have.

## Appendix 2.2  Self-assessment list

*Self-assessment project*

JAPN 1201-001, Fall 2005

Name:_____

1. Write what you've done in learning Japanese using ellipses: Workbook→WB, Textbook→Txt,   Reading→R, Writing journal→J, Speaking→S, Learning kanji→K, Learning Vocab. →V   Listening tape→Au, CALL→CALL, Meeting LA→LA, Others→Other

2. Evaluate your learning in the previous week using ellipses:

    Well Done!! 70–100%→ ☺ ; So-so: 40–69%→Δ; No comment: 0–39%→X

3. Write problems/comments/learning strategies.

| Week | Chapter test/ quiz | 1 What you've done in learning Japanese in previous week? | 2 Evaluation | 3 Problems/ comments/ learning strategies | Feedback from instructor |
|---|---|---|---|---|---|
| **Wk1** 8/22 8/26 | | | | | |
| **Wk2** 8/29 9/2 | Quiz1 Quiz2 | | | | |
| **Wk3** 9/5 9/9 | Ch1&2 Test Kanji Q | 9/5 **(M) Labor Day** | | | |

## Appendix 2.3 Self-assessment project questionnaire (questions only)

Use the scale below to answer the questions. If you think the statement is more or less true of you, find the number between 1 and 5 that best describes you and **CIRCLE** it.

| "Self-assessment list" was helpful in: | Strongly Agree | Agree | Neutral | Disagree | Strongly Disagree |
|---|---|---|---|---|---|
| 1. Reviewing my Japanese learning regarding *what* I did each week. | 5 | 4 | 3 | 2 | 1 |
| 2. Assessing the achievement of my own performance each week. | 5 | 4 | 3 | 2 | 1 |
| 3. Reflecting my own learning each week. | 5 | 4 | 3 | 2 | 1 |
| 4. Writing in the Self-assessment list is troublesome. | 5 | 4 | 3 | 2 | 1 |
| 5. Writing in the Self-assessment list each week is waste of time. | 5 | 4 | 3 | 2 | 1 |
| 6. Feedback received from my teacher is helpful. | 5 | 4 | 3 | 2 | 1 |

Would you recommend the use of the "Self-assessment list" in spring, 2006?    Yes    No

Please comment on the "Self-assessment list."

# 3 Utilizing peer teaching and tutoring to decrease attrition rates

## 3.1 Introduction

This chapter introduces two strategies, a language assistant program and a peer tutoring program, integrated into the Japanese program at UNC Charlotte to lessen the poverty of opportunity and interest, thereby reducing attrition rates. The language assistants were integrated into Japanese classes using Japanese native speakers and returnees from studying abroad in Japan, and the peer tutoring program was implemented in elementary and intermediate classes with higher-level students who could help them by offering one or two individualized study sessions per week with struggling students.

## 3.2 Introducing language assistant programs to solve the poverty of opportunity

Language Assistant (henceforth, LA) programs can help minor FL learners overcome the poverty of opportunity problem, which is imperative for learners to improve their target language skills and maintain their motivation, as argued in Chapters 1 and 2. LAs can increase opportunities for practice both in and outside of the classroom when a program is properly implemented, as described in this chapter.

Teaching assistants and teaching practicum courses have become ubiquitous in academic higher education in the United States. Teaching practicums generally last for one week (Willard-Holt, 2001), three weeks (Ozek, 2009; Sakai, 1995), or two months (Sahin, 2008), with the purpose of imparting teaching methods to participants through real-life practice and are often required to earn a teacher's license or receive credit toward becoming a teacher in the future. Many universities in the United States also have a system by which students can assist instructors with classes, in laboratories, or in other ways. Usually offered to graduate students, these positions are widely known as teaching assistants (henceforth, TAs) (D'Andrea, 1996; Korinek, Howard, & Bridges, 1999; Kost, 2008; Mewis, Dee, Lam, Obdradovich, & Cassidy, 2018). TAs play an important role in undergraduate learning (Mewis et al., 2018) and are "central figures in academia" (Korinek et al., 1999, p. 344). For example, Mewis et al. (2018) reported that 91% of the biology laboratory courses were taught by TAs in the 34 large research schools in the United States. TA work often includes not only laboratory assistance but also many academic and administrative tasks (Güller, Keskin, Döyen, & Akyer, 2015), participating in all aspects of teaching, for example, preparing lesson plans, teaching classes under the supervision of the instructor, grading student tests or quizzes, answering students' questions, participating in the administration of oral exams, and designing and grading written exams (Kost, 2008; Murray, 1996). Sometimes they even work as replacements for instructors (Korinek et al., 1999). TAs are generally paid per hour, and the positions serve both as a source of financial support for postgraduate students, and as a teaching source for academic institutions (D'Andrea, 1996).

Although the general concept of helping with classes is the same, the LA program implemented in the Japanese program at UNC Charlotte differs in several important ways. LAs here help to foster strong and long-lasting bonds between themselves and the learners and are considered members of their assigned language classes who help learners to overcome the poverty of opportunity, and also encourage them to continue studying. This section introduces my vision of a successful LA program, describes the underlying theory behind it, explains how it differs from traditional TAs, and gives an example of a case study (Kato, 2018b) from the Japanese program at UNC Charlotte, and reports the outcomes through three kinds of participant reflections: (1) Japanese LA opinions (observed by questionnaires and reflection papers), (2) instructor assessments (written papers), and (3) US LA perceptions (questionnaires and reflection papers). Finally, recommendations are provided for creating such a program at other institutions based on this study.

### 3.2.1 *A case study of an LA program that differs from traditional TAs*

There are three primary differences between LAs in the Japanese program at UNC Charlotte and TAs. First, the eligibility of LAs are different. Eligible LAs are set as Japanese study abroad students, returnees from studying abroad in Japan for one academic year, and advanced US learners of Japanese. The Japanese program in 2019 offers four levels of language classes: (1) elementary I and II, (2) intermediate I and II, (3) upper intermediate I and II, and (4) advanced courses. LAs are assigned to one of the first three levels (but not to advanced classes) and attend classes with the learners four days a week. For most Japanese study abroad students, it is their first time to teach Japanese in English and thus their primary task is to learn how Japanese is taught in the United States.

The second biggest difference between TAs and LAs are their roles in the classrooms. Although TAs often take a more traditional role with distance between themselves and students, LAs are expected to have close relationships with students and instructors, partnering with the instructor in demonstrating dialogues, supervising learners in activities and pair or group work, proctoring chapter tests, delivering and collecting papers for class quizzes, and collecting and checking homework assignments. Furthermore, LAs are required to give two teaching practicums per semester. Additionally, while TAs often assist instructors by marking tests and managing student scores, LAs are not allowed to do so because they often become close with the students.[1] Moreover, although TAs are usually paid per hour for their work, LAs receive credit hours for fulfilling their tasks instead of monetary compensation.

Finally, LAs' tasks also carry over outside of the class hours with activities such as "LA sessions," which are held twice per semester for 15 minutes with each student in the assigned class. LAs meet and communicate face to face with each learner individually in LA sessions. During LA sessions, LAs ask questions for review and practice, respond to student question(s), and converse with them in Japanese. Before these sessions, instructors provide LAs with questions that include grammar points that students have studied in the class. LAs keep brief records of each session conducted with each learner and submit them to their instructor after finishing all sessions. LAs also participate in Japanese program events outside of the classroom, such as yearly speech contests and "Year-End Presentations" (see Chapter 5). LAs help students who plan to participate in speech contests by giving them pointers and helping them improve their speech outside of the class-hours, and assist students who will perform in Year-End Presentations with the linguistic aspects of their presentations and sometimes perform with them.

### 3.2.1.1 Implementing the LA program at UNC Charlotte

In the 2016 fall semester, a course titled JAPN 3400 "Teaching Practicum" was offered for the first time within the Japanese language curriculum at UNC Charlotte. Prior to this, students could function as LAs only by registering for an independent study course.[2] A course credit contract between LAs and instructors was created and shown to LAs registered for the independent study course in advance, and a syllabus based on it was created for the new Teaching Practicum course (see Appendix 3.1). There were not enough LAs in the past to provide one for every Japanese language class, so they were offered primarily for elementary level classes and intermediate level classes if there were enough LAs. However, with ever an increasing number of Japanese students studying abroad at UNC Charlotte and US students who returned from studying abroad in Japan and want to become LAs, a larger pool of potential LAs became available from 2016, and the need to create a course to train LAs arose, resulting in the offering of the "Teaching Practicum" course.

Japanese study abroad students were recruited for the Teaching Practicum course by advertising it to all expected exchange partner university students via email. There were 20 LAs registered for the Teaching Practicum course in the fall semester of 2016, consisting of 16 Japanese study abroad students and 4 returnees from study abroad programs in Japan in 2016. Twelve Japanese language classes were offered that semester, so two LAs were assigned to classes with over 20 students enrolled in them, and one LA was assigned to classes with fewer than 19. All students who registered for the Teaching Practicum class were assigned to a Japanese language class, attended an orientation, and had a meeting with their instructors before they commenced their duties and read the Teaching Practicum course syllabus.

I began the LA program as the coordinator of the Japanese program and modified it in the manner described earlier to help learners overcome the poverty of opportunity problem mentioned at several points in this book. The addition of one or two LAs to each class allowed them to have more opportunities to interact with native speakers both in and outside the class hours and instructors seemed pleased to have assistants in every class-hour as it allowed for more student engagement. However, there was still no clear indication that the LAs themselves found their roles beneficial to themselves or that they were amenable to the conditions. Therefore, I examined their views on how beneficial they felt the LA program was to themselves through surveys and reflection papers regarding their roles and duties.

### 3.2.2 The effects of LA duties on LAs and the program

Questionnaires were given to LAs who participated in the 2016 Teaching Practicum course to evaluate how they viewed the course and its implementation into Japanese classes. LAs were also asked to write reflection papers, which were analyzed through a conceptually clustered matrix analysis (Kato, 2018b; Miles & Huberman, 1944), and opinions were collected from the class instructors. All LAs ($N = 20$) responded to the questionnaires and submitted their reflection papers.

#### 3.2.2.1 LAs' perspectives of the LA program (questionnaires and reflection papers)

The questionnaires were distributed prior to the latter half of the semester when all LAs had performed both the LA session and the teaching practicum. According to the results, most LAs (85%) strongly agreed or agreed with three questions regarding their experiences through being an LA: (1) whether the course was as they expected, (2) whether the students' attitudes in the class were excellent, and (3) whether they could make friends through the LA program. Furthermore, many LAs (75%) strongly agreed or agreed that they enjoyed the LA session, and reported that they could get to know the students in their classes better than before conducting the sessions. Over half of the LAs responded that it became easier for them to conduct the class activities after their first LA session and that they were looking forward to the second one. Though there was concern about whether or not the LAs would dislike the LA sessions because of the amount of time required outside of class hours, no LAs reported having such feelings.

LAs also answered two questions regarding the teaching practicums favorably, with approximately two thirds agreeing that they were looking forward to second one and only one LA viewing the classroom teaching practicum unfavorably. This LA wrote that she was terribly nervous about teaching in front of others due to her lack of English ability, leading her to feel she did not teach well. However, in her reflection paper from the end of the semester, she reported having made lesson plans by herself for her second teaching practicum, and although she felt nervous at the beginning of the teaching demonstration, her nervousness gradually disappeared because she was familiar with the students in her class, allowing her to enjoy the second teaching experience. She commented that it was, ultimately, "an amazing experience."

All LAs ($N = 20$) submitted reflection papers with the assigned title, "What I learned through being an LA" in either English or Japanese at the end of the semester, that is, what they learned through the course and what experiences they felt would be useful in the future. The majority of LAs' (80%) perceptions of the program were positive and they expressed pleasure with the experience in representative comments such as, "I had a priceless experience because teaching Japanese to Americans at the university could not have happened for me" and "[it was] a precious asset in my life." Although many found it difficult to teach (45%), over one-third of LAs wrote that they learned valuable lessons because they experienced so many things, such as teaching a class, for the first time. One-quarter of LAs thus reported that being an LA was a worthwhile and "fantastic" experience.

One quarter of LAs were impressed with US students' active attitudes in class, saying that they were "serious and enthusiastic toward learning Japanese," "ask questions if they are unclear" and "state their opinions in a dignified manner without being afraid of failure." As Japan has a collectivistic society, students are inculcated from a young age to prioritize being a good member of society and listening passively to the teacher is generally seen as the best method to learn, which makes Japanese students tend to be passive in class (Stone, 2012), which is likely why they were surprised and inspired by this. Over one-third of LAs were fond of the Japanese class that they were assigned to, writing comments such as "I always looked forward to attending the class," and one LA writing that she "terribly missed the class" after it was over.

## 58  Utilizing peer teaching

Over one-third of the LAs found the teaching practicum difficult and said that it made them nervous, writing, "it was much more difficult than I expected" and "it was the most tough experience [for me] since I was really poor at speaking in front of people." However, regardless of the difficulty, they also reported this experience turned out to be very useful and they found they had improved at their shortcomings through the activity.

LAs seemed to enjoy their LA sessions, with some describing them as "the happiest time" in their study abroad experience. Some were impressed with students' attitudes since they "try to understand and solve their problems through my explanation in English." LAs discovered various aspects of the students' personalities, become closer to them and found it easier to engage in social interactions with them afterwards. Some LAs even noted that they wanted to have more LA sessions.

### 3.2.2.2 Instructors' opinions of the LA program

Five instructors' opinions of the LA program were taken, and were all found to be extremely positive, likely because the program is highly advantageous for them. All of the instructors welcomed with the idea of having at least one LA in their language classes. Their opinions can be categorized into four ideas:

#### 3.2.2.2.1 ADVANTAGES TO HAVING JAPANESE STUDY ABROAD STUDENTS AS LAS

Instructors liked having Japanese study abroad students as LAs because their students generally do not have opportunities to listen to or communicate in Japanese outside of their instructors, and the LA program afforded them another opportunity to use the language. Instructors noted that some students found it easier to speak with the LA rather than themselves because the LAs were closer in age, which made students feel more relaxed, which corresponds with studies by Moust and Schmidt (1994) and Hilsdon (2014). Students also felt LA sessions to be more authentic because they could speak directly with Japanese native speakers. Furthermore, LAs became easily aware of problems that students had due increased contact with them outside of the class-hours and could help instructors by reporting the problems to them so that they could then give a review of the difficult points in class or help the troubled student(s) individually. Instructors also reported that the LAs work participating in out-of-class event in the Japanese program was also helpful because it reduced their own workload in this respect. Lastly, by spending time with the same class for a whole semester, Japanese study abroad students created strong friendships with US students that encouraged more study abroad exchanges, as US students wanted to go to Japan to meet their LAs again.

#### 3.2.2.2.2 ADVANTAGES WITHIN THE CLASS-HOUR

Instructors noted that assistants were beneficial during the class-hour, as they could supervise students, assist with explanations of exercises, help instructors with quizzes and tests, and give feedback on assignments, which allowed them to focus on teaching and managing classwork more smoothly. For example, while the instructors were explaining the elements of kanji characters, the LAs could check students' writing by moving around the class and pointing out errors in the students' notes promptly, increasing student engagement.

#### 3.2.2.2.3 ADVANTAGES OUTSIDE OF CLASS-HOURS

Instructors also mentioned that LAs were beneficial to students outside of the class-hours. They commented that US students seemed to communicate with LAs a lot outside of class, which allowed them to acquire various daily expressions that they didn't or couldn't learn during the class-hour. Furthermore, LAs checked students' homework assignments, which instructors noted as the greatest assistance because of how much time it saved them, allowing them to spend more time preparing lessons for classes.

#### 3.2.2.2.4 ADVANTAGES FOR THE JAPANESE STUDY ABROAD STUDENTS THEMSELVES

Instructors also noted that LAs were able to make friends in the class and subsequently improve their English abilities. One common problem for Japanese study abroad students is that once abroad, they tend to form groups of only other Japanese students because of their language barrier and end up not communicating with the local university students, returning to Japan without having made significant gains in their English ability (Kato, 2016). However, LAs attend class with US students and are required to be active in helping instructors and local students, so these activities seemed to help them gain confidence in their ability to communicate with US university students. Furthermore, some instructors noted that LAs also learned valuable class management and teaching skills.

### 3.2.2.3 *Returnee LAs' opinions of the LA program*

Four US students who had returned from studying abroad in Japan became LAs in 2016 along with several of the Japanese study abroad students. Their opinions were gathered as representative of US learners' views toward the LA program. These four LAs were required to write their opinions of the LA program and also submitted questionnaires. Questionnaire responses from the four students indicated that they all (100%) strongly agreed or agreed with the statements that being an LA fulfilled their expectations, they had confidence that they could assist their instructors as an LA, and found many friends through being an LA. Although three out of four students (75%) were nervous about the teaching practicum, none found it difficult, and 75% looked forward to the second one. In their reflection papers, all of them wrote that being an LA was a good experience in comments such as, "being an LA has been extraordinary experience for me," "the most challenging. ... As much hard work as it was I enjoyed every minute of it." One student noted that, "The presentations went so well that I may consider becoming a teacher sometime in the future."

They also commented on their own experiences having been provided with a Japanese LA in the past. They noted that they learned many things from the LAs such as Japanese culture and less-common Japanese slang and colloquialisms. They remembered wanting to communicate with their LAs both in and outside of class-hours and wanted to become one themselves. This indicates that LAs contributed to solving the poverty of opportunity for them. One commented that he was pleased to meet his former LA in Japan when he went to study abroad, and noted how important such relationships are.

Furthermore, some US learners in the Japanese classes noted that they were impressed with the Japanese skills of returnee LAs. These LAs carried out their duties entirely in Japanese and advised students about their future prospects of learning Japanese based on their own experiences. Many such students were inspired by the returnee LAs and mentioned wanting to become an LA themselves some day. They also noted that they were encouraged to study abroad and felt more driven to continue learning Japanese and obtain a Japanese minor or BA degree.

Finally, LAs noted that they themselves learned a lot by reviewing Japanese grammar in the classes that they already learned in the past and it was a great review for them because they could understand it more deeply than the time they learned it by noting, "I was relearning things that I couldn't remember, which allowed me to improve my writing skills ... repetition is the only way to truly understand the Japanese language." This corresponds with many researchers (e.g., Christensen, Schmalz, Challyandra, & Stark, 2018; Topping, 1996) who suggest that teaching is a good way to review and learn.

### 3.2.3 Conclusions from the case study

This section explored how Japanese study abroad students and returnee students viewed the experience of being an LA as part of a structured course. The outcomes suggested that the LA experience for Japanese study abroad students turned out to be a meaningful and beneficial one in their lives (Kato, 2018b). Most were delighted to attend their Japanese language classes, felt fortunate to be able to make many US friends because of it, and enjoyed the interpersonal communication that was a part of the program. Specifically, LA sessions were found to help Japanese LAs become closer to the students in their assigned class, which aided them in their duties. Japanese LAs also gained sociocultural awareness, as they were also impressed with the US students' learning attitudes, which hopefully influenced them to develop a more active learning style themselves.

Prior to the study, there were three concerns with this program: (1) would LAs accept the LA session task conducted outside of the class-hours, (2) would the burden of correcting students' homework assignments be too great for LAs, and (3) how would LAs view the required two teaching practicums? However, neither the first or second concern seemed to be an issue when LAs were surveyed after finishing their duties. LAs acknowledged that the experience of having been an LA was valuable, regardless of them feeling the amount of duties to be outside the class-hours and overwhelming at first. They noted that after overcoming the workload, they gained significant knowledge through the program, and would like to apply what they learned in the future. Although some LAs reported that teaching practicum was difficult and made them nervous at first, later they found it to be an advantageous and worthwhile experience because they would not have otherwise had such an opportunity.

Instructors were particularly positive toward the LA program because of how it helped to solve the poverty of opportunity problem that many of their students suffered from (Kato, 2018b). They noted that the program provided their students with exposure to Japanese native speakers or advanced students similar in age, which provided them with more opportunities for communication. They were of the opinion that the LAs greatly influenced their students, who could receive information about Japanese language and culture directly from them. They found numerous advantages to the LA program, and were very welcoming of it, pointing to the help they received within the class-hours, and the merit of having LAs communicate with students outside of the class-hours as well.

US learners who studied Japanese with LAs in the past and returned from Japan after studying abroad were enthusiastic about the opportunity to become an LA. Most US students welcomed the duties, had studied with Japanese LAs in the past and were eager to become an LA themselves. They tried to mimic LAs who had encouraged them to continue studying Japanese in the past and enhance the motivation of the students that they worked with and encourage them to study abroad themselves. In this way, having prior experience of studying Japanese with an LA was found to greatly influence and foster US students' motivation to study Japanese (Kato, 2018b).

This study suggested that the LA program is win-win-win in that all of those who participated in this intervention, that is, language learners, LAs and instructors, reported it as beneficial to themselves and the language students.

### 3.2.4 Advice for creating and implementing LA programs

An LA program such as the one described in this chapter can increase opportunities for language learners to communicate in their TL and motivate them, alleviating the poverty of opportunity, and to some extent, the poverty of interest. While this is important for any FL instructor, this is especially critical for teachers of minor FLs because of the inherent lack of opportunities that their students face.

Although it might seem very challenging to implement an LA program at one's own institution, it is surely feasible. In my own case, I had been using and training LAs for years until it became possible to find enough LAs that I could create a teaching practicum course that has been systematically offered since 2016. While having a systemized course for the LAs themselves is ideal, instructors who wish to create an LA program of their own may have to start small and work toward this goal as I did. Those who would like to implement an LA program in their own language program should consider the following:

First, LAs can be found in a number of ways. My first suggestion is to try to find native-speaking study abroad students, as with the case study given in this section. Having LAs who are close in age to the students helps them feel more comfortable, which provides additional motivation. It is easiest to incentivize such LAs with things such as course credit, but if no such students are available, you may be able to find other native speakers who are undergraduate and graduate students, researchers or research assistants at your institution who may also be willing to join classes as an LA. Finally, in the case that there are no native speakers of the language available to help, please remember that while native speakers are ideal, advanced students from the program can also act as LAs for lower-level classes, as reported in the case study. This can be especially beneficial when such students have spent time studying abroad in a country that speaks the target language.

Second, if there are not enough LAs to offer a teaching practicum course, instructors can often create independent courses so that their LAs can receive some course credit. For LA programs, a win-win situation works best, so I recommend avoiding volunteer LAs. Although the sentiment may be nice, LAs have a number of duties and responsibilities, and it is difficult for volunteers to maintain enough motivation to properly participate and assist throughout an entire semester without any sort of compensation.

Third, I recommend holding an orientation session before assigning LAs to classes. LAs need to be aware of what their duties and responsibilities are, and a supervisor should check to make sure they are eager to perform them before assigning them to a class. The class rules, expectations, and manners of LAs need to be explained in detail in the orientation as duties may be different depending on the institution and situation (e.g., no eating meals or using cellphones during the class-hours, wearing professional clothing, no inappropriate meeting times or places during LA sessions, etc.). Finally, if potential LAs are uncomfortable with the guidelines of the work, they should be recommended to drop out from the beginning, as it could potentially be demotivating to students if they are made to believe that they will have an LA only to have the LA quit after a short period of time, or if students find themselves with an LA who is uncommitted to their work.

Finally, someone at the institution should be designated as the coordinator for the LA program. The person in charge should handle the important, but difficult and time-consuming, background tasks such as advertising the program, recruiting LAs, providing course registration information, ensuring some sort of benefit or compensation for LAs (such as course credit), assigning LAs to individual language classes, and providing them with an orientation. As all of these tasks occur at the beginning of the semester, the Japanese program at UNC Charlotte does not count the LA teaching practicum class toward the instructor's teaching load. Thus, the supervisor of the LA program should be aware that even if a teaching practicum or independent study course is created, the LAs might receive course credit, but the instructor will often not and thus must volunteer their time in this regard. However, considering the great advantages for the students, LAs, and language instructors, it is a worthwhile undertaking.

### 3.3 Peer tutor programs to save struggling learners

Battling the poverty of interest problem can be especially difficult for teachers of minor FLs and yet is very important, as they usually cannot afford to have high attrition rates amongst students if they are to keep their programs and classes from being cancelled. While instructors obviously do their best to pay close attention to all of their students, there are always some who concern them. Instructors will want students to not only continue to take more advanced classes in the future, but also prevent registered students from withdrawing from courses. As improving these numbers is vital to maintaining a healthy language program, the Japanese program at UNC Charlotte began implementing a peer tutoring program from the fall semester of 2011, in order to assist students at risk of failing or withdrawing and keep them motivated until the end of the semester. Upon the first iteration of this new intervention process, there was a student who concerned me almost immediately from the beginning of the semester. The student had failed an elementary Spanish language class, and decided to take Japanese to fulfill her language requirement for graduation. Her choice astonished me because Spanish is much easier for native English speakers to learn than Japanese, so I was worried that she wouldn't be able to pass the class to fulfill her language requirement. I found an advanced learner who was volunteered to study together with her. She was pleased with this arrangement and received support from the advanced learner twice per week throughout the semester. Due to this intervention, she was able to learn enough to receive a grade of "D" and successfully graduate.

Based on this experience and the fact that students may be at risk of withdrawing from any class regardless of the passion of the teacher or presence of support programs such as an LA program or self-assessment and feedback approach, a peer tutoring program was implemented as a structured arrangement into the Japanese program to improve student performance. It was targeted at those considered to be at risk, as per Hilsdon (2014), and found to be generally successful. This section describes the work done to establish the peer tutoring program in the Japanese program at UNC Charlotte and gives advice to those who wish to implement a similar approach at their own institution.

### 3.3.1 Peer tutoring in the literature

Peer tutoring is a method that is certainly nothing new or innovative. In fact, it can be traced back in some form or another to the days of ancient Greece (Topping, 1996). The fine details of peer tutoring have been tweaked over the years, as can be seen in a number of studies, including those on peer instruction and near-peer instruction (Lee, 1998; Lockspeiser, O'Sullivan, Teherani, & Muller, 2008; Moust & Schmidt, 1994; Topping, 1996), but in all cases, there are many similar advantages for students who receive support from their peers. According to Topping (1996), tutees in such programs often become "more active, interactive and participative [in their own] learning, immediate feedback, swift prompting, [and exhibit] lowered anxiety" (p. 325). Lee (1998) has also reported that peer tutoring increases student retention and reduces withdrawal rates. Students who need motivational scaffolding are often calm, quiet and have few friends, so learning sessions with peers who are similar in age helps to mitigate their social isolation, which can in turn boost motivation as well as social learning (Topping, 1996).

While this might be helpful with any subject and in the tutees lives in general, it could be particularly helpful with studying FLs, as the social constructivist theory of language learning suggests that language is only truly acquired through social interaction (Gergen, 1999; Hilsdon, 2014; Vygotsky, 1978). Moust and Schmidt (1994) and Hilsdon (2014) suggest that social interaction is increased with peer tutors, noting that tutees prefer peer tutoring to individual instructor attention because they feel their peers understand their problems better, are more interested in their lives, and are not as authoritarian. Peer tutoring can also greatly aide instructors, as they can devote more of their time to preparation and planning work while still being assured that each student is getting enough individual attention.

Another advantage to peer tutoring is that tutors themselves learn, review their own learning process, and boost their own motivation through helping others learn. For example, Topping (1996) claims that peer tutoring can be considered "learning by teaching," and compares it to the old saying, "to teach is to learn twice" (p. 324). Furthermore, motivational scaffolding from peer tutors has been found to positively impact both tutees and tutors, improving their attitudes in class (e.g., Christensen et al., 2018; Topping, 1996). For example, Hilsdon (2014) investigated a peer-tutor program introduced in a higher education institution where tutor sessions were held weekly with two leaders and found that the leaders perceived their benefits in helping to be all related to their own intrinsic motivation, such as: pride as a leader, the advantage as soon-to-be a job-seekers as teachers, it being good for their CVs, increased confidence, and consolidated learning.

Because of the mutually beneficial nature of peer tutoring, the practice is not uncommon in a number of subjects (e.g., Bailey & Vooheris-Sargent, 2018; Christensen et al., 2018; Gerena & Keiler, 2012; Ryder, Russell, Burton, Quinn, & Daly, 2017; Youngs & Green, 2001), and is used from lower levels of education, that is, high school summer programs (Gerena & Keiler, 2012) to higher education. One advantage to these programs is that they seem to reduce attrition rates, such as reported in Gerena and Keiler (2012), who found that when peer tutoring was introduced, high school graduation rates for students who once failed their final graduation exams raised by 20%. Peer tutoring has also been noted to help in foreign language, such as in Youngs and Green (2001), who reported on peer assistants whose purpose was to enhance tutee's writing ability in seven kinds of FLs in their language department. Participants in this study noted that out-of-class peer review was beneficial to them and also the writing assistants themselves recognized that their writing skills had improved through working with their peers.

Although there is substantial evidence and several studies which suggest that peer tutoring is effective in supporting learning and teaching, Topping (1996) pointed out some issues that must be considered when creating a peer tutoring program, namely, that organizing a peer tutoring system is time-consuming, selecting appropriate peer tutors is laborious, and appropriately matching tutors and tutees can be especially challenging.

### 3.3.2 A case study of peer tutoring in the Japanese program at UNC Charlotte

Because students in any class can be in need of support through motivational scaffolding, but minor FL learners are disproportionally affected by poverty of interest, it is especially important for at-risk minor FL students to receive extra support not only from instructors, LAs, and self-assessment interventions but also through regular, interpersonal sessions once or twice per week until the end of the semester. Therefore, a peer tutoring system was introduced into the Japanese program at UNC Charlotte, and was carefully observed to see its effects on at-risk students.

### 3.3.2.1 Procedures

Upon implementing the peer tutoring system, instructors in the Japanese program at UNC Charlotte teaching classes beyond the initial three semesters recruited peer tutors from their classes soon after starting each new semester, and asked them to apply by registering through an application form. Upon receiving the forms from tutor volunteers, instructors uploaded their information, such as their names, telephone numbers, email addresses, available times for tutoring session, and courses able to teach onto a designated website that all Japanese instructors at UNC Charlotte could access. Table 3.1 shows an example of the list of information about tutors and tutees uploaded on the designated website.

Simultaneously, instructors of lower-level classes asked if there were any requests for peer tutors. After receiving requests, instructors seeking peer tutors for their students went to the designated website and found appropriate tutors based mainly on the tutor's level and both students' available times. Upon finding an appropriate tutor, they input the tutee's current course level, desired session times, and instructor's name in the ninth box of the website.

The tutee's instructor became responsible for organizing tutoring sessions by getting in contact with tutors, tutees and the tutors' instructors, which was generally done by email. The tutee's instructor also printed a "Peer Tutor Log" (see Appendix 3.2) and gave it to the tutor. As soon as the tutee's instructor had received a confirmation email from the tutor, tutoring sessions began. The number of sessions was determined by the participants, but most had sessions once a week, depending on the tutee's needs and the tutor's availability. Some pairs had over 20 sessions per

*Table 3.1* Peer tutor list in a designated website with example entry

| 1. J. Class | 2. Instructor | 3. Students' name | 4. E-mail | 5. Cellphone # | 6. Available days, times and place to meet |
|---|---|---|---|---|---|
| JAPN 1201 | ****** | ****** | ***@uncc.edu | 704-***-**** | MW3:00-5:00, R after 4:30 @ library |
| 7. Courses able to teach | 8. Comments by instructor (skills, experience, etc.) | | 9. Tutee/instructor's names, course, desired session times | | 10. Times of sessions |
| Up to 2202 | Study abroad 1 yr, kind, punctual | | ***, **** 1201, M/W 4:00 | | # times |

Note: ***To be filled by the participant.

semester, while others only met a few times. Sessions were monitored simply by having tutors keep a "Peer Tutor Log" in which they record information about each tutor session, such as the dates, times, and a summary of the content they studied together. The tutors then submitted the log to the tutee's instructor at the end of the semester. The tutee's instructor input the number of sessions held during the semester into the tenth question box in Table 3.1.

### 3.3.3 Effects of the peer tutor program at UNC Charlotte

Students who studied with a peer tutor were generally able to avoid failing or withdrawing, earning at least a grade of "D," some of them even receiving a "C." In one of the first years of the peer tutoring intervention at UNC Charlotte, one tutor reported that it was extremely difficult for his tutee to remember even very basic grammar points or Japanese characters. Even though he repeatedly taught the characters or points, his tutee simply could not remember them. Therefore, he always started every session by reviewing the basic fundamentals. Despite having several sessions per week, it took a tremendous amount of time to review all of the characters and grammar. However, through this level of repetition the tutee could fortunately pass the class with a grade of "D." The extraordinary patience of the tutor was greatly appreciated and fortunately the tutee did not withdraw or fail the course. Without the tutor's extensive support, this particular tutee likely would not have passed the course.

Peer tutors do not receive any money or credit hours, and are purely volunteers. The instructors in the Japanese program appreciated the tutors and expressed their gratitude instead by acknowledging tutors who held at least five tutorial sessions during the semester on stage with service awards in the Japanese program's Year-End Presentations ceremonies. Six students who had helped as tutors were introduced, handed a certificate of appreciation (see Appendix 3.3) and received a round of applause in the fall semester of 2011. Thus, it seems that the program at least contributed to keeping six students from failing or withdrawing from their courses.

#### 3.3.3.1 Benefits for peer tutors themselves

As with the LAs introduced in the previous section of this chapter and also presented earlier in the literature review (Christensen et al., 2018; Hilsdon, 2014; Ryder et al., 2017; Topping, 1996; Youngs & Green, 2001), peer tutors themselves can also learn and enhance their own motivation by helping to teach their peers. For example, tutors reported that they had to clearly explain every element of Japanese language to their tutees, so they had to ensure that they knew the content very well and got a review of Japanese grammar in the process. Different from LAs, peer tutors concentrate on assisting only one tutee, especially students who are struggling to learn

68  *Utilizing peer teaching*

Japanese, so they need to be patient in teaching, as exemplified in the earlier section. In this way, tutoring can also help them to build a sense of perseverance. Moreover, being a tutor can also bring joy to the tutors themselves when they see their tutee's pleasure after achieving their goals thanks to their assistance.

Another benefit for peer tutors is that they can use the experience as a tutor in their curriculum vitae, which can help them when looking for jobs in the future (Hilsdon, 2014). While this is important for any student who is looking to go into teaching in the future, it is especially important for students of Japanese at UNC Charlotte because one popular job postgraduation for our students is assistant language teacher (henceforth, ALT) in Japan. These job openings generally prefer candidates with some practical teaching experience, so students who are interested in such opportunities after graduation are generally eager to volunteer as tutors in order to fulfill this requirement. In fact, some students at UNC Charlotte who did LA or peer tutoring work reported that the experience helped them get a job as an ALT, and also practically when performing their duties once they began working at schools in Japan.

Furthermore, society in general places great value on doing volunteer work. Even if a student is not interested in becoming a teacher in the future, having clearly done volunteer work can help students to progress into a wide variety of postgraduate degree programs and job opportunities. Thus, becoming a tutor can potentially help them with their own careers, or advancing in their life in general.

### 3.3.4  Conclusions from the case study

This section introduced how implementing a peer tutoring program in the Japanese program at UNC Charlotte helped students who needed or sought help studying and lowered the number of students that failed or quit classes. Since the program's implementation, instructors have tried to identify at-risk students as early as possible at the start of each new semester and to arrange peer tutors for them. Since integrating this strategy in 2011, it has been employed every semester and improved student learning academically to assist alleviating the poverty of interest. While such a program is applicable for any type of learning, but it is especially helpful for minor FL learners because of the poverty of interest that they generally face.

### 3.3.5  Advice for integrating peer tutor programs

I highly recommend implementing a peer tutor program at every institution because there are always some students that concern instructors and require extra attention that they cannot always provide. However, there are four considerations when establishing a peer tutor program:

First, when recruiting tutors, it is best to explain the merits of becoming a peer tutor, for example, the importance of and value in conducting volunteer activities, the merits of having teaching experience if they'd like to be a teacher in the future, and how they can learn the language better themselves by teaching it. Because the tutors will likely be strictly volunteers, it is important to motivate them to do their best, and one good way to do this is simply to explain the benefits that tutoring has for the tutors.

Second, tutors generally have a greater sense of responsibility than tutees (being more motivated students to begin with), so it is wise to ask tutors, rather than tutees, to keep track of any peer tutoring records that you would like to request. It is best to reduce the burden on the already struggling tutees as much as possible, so if you would like to implement a peer tutoring record, I would advise giving any related tasks to the tutor.

Third, though the tutor can be asked to do some tasks in addition to teaching, for example, completing a tutoring record, the responsibility for the majority of the managerial aspects related to the peer tutoring should lie with the tutee's instructor, for example, selecting a peer tutor, contacting both the tutor and his/her instructor, and so on. Furthermore, the tutee's instructor should also provide the tutor with any log that will be requested for program records before commencing the tutorial sessions. As Topping (1996) pointed out, matching tutors and tutees can be difficult, so the tutee's instructor should also carefully consider who to ask to become their students' tutors. Such consideration can be done with the help of online resources, such as the web form that is used at UNC Charlotte, as introduced earlier.

Lastly, it is best to start peer tutor sessions as early as possible in the semester, as timing is critical. If you offer support too late, it will be too difficult for struggling students to catch up with the class, which can lead them to withdraw from or fail the class despite their tutor's efforts.

## Appendix 3.1 Syllabus of "Teaching Practicum" course (content only)

**Course description**: This course provides students as *Language Assistant (LA)* with the opportunity to acquire and develop teaching skills and methods through working with/for their assigned instructor and students. LA will help learners in his/her assigned class to develop their four Japanese language competencies (listening, speaking, reading and writing) plus grammar. This course provides students as LA with the opportunity to assist fellow students' language learning by sharing their cultural experience (study abroad experience and/or extracurricular activities, as well as foreign language learning strategies etc.) with the learners. Furthermore, LA is required to conduct teaching demonstrations twice during a semester.

In addition, this course will facilitate Japanese study abroad students' adjustment to a new environment through being a member of one Japanese language course where Japanese language learners would like to communicate with LA.

- *Orientation* will be held @ **COED 103 at 8:00am on August 22 (W)**.
- *Note:* After the orientation, your class meeting time will be that of your assigned Japanese language course.
- *Mid-semester session* will be held @ **COED 103 at 8:00am on October 3 (W)**.

**Requirements:** As goals of this course, students are required to:

- Attend each class meeting and join class activities.
- Help students in their assigned class to develop their language skills as well as expand their knowledge of Japan and Japanese culture.
- Observe and learn the teaching methods employed by the assigned instructor.
- Collect and provide feedback on students' homework assignments.
- Conduct LA sessions conversing in Japanese outside the class-hour twice a semester.
- Assist the instructor of their assigned class whenever needed during the class-hour.
- Have a good relationship with the instructor and the students in their assigned class.
- Write a reflection paper on what you have learned through the course and what aspects you will be able to make use in the future from your experience of being LA.

**Course information via Internet:** You are RESPONSIBLE to check your UNC Charlotte email accounts in order to know any changes of the course and our *CANVAS site* (http://canvas.uncc.edu), and also to know various info on the events conducted in the Japanese program (http://unccjapn.blogspot.com/).

**Reflection paper:** You are required to submit a reflection paper with the topic, "*What I learned through being LA,*" in either English or Japanese. Due date is the last class-hour of the semester (*2 pages double-spaced with a type font in 12-point size*): i.e., **Dec. 5 (W), 2018**. Submit it to *your instructor*.

**Attendance:** Class attendance is mandatory and punctuality is required. In the case that you are unable to attend the class due to some unexpected illness or injury, first get contact with *your* *instructor* ASAP to let him/her know about your absence and submit an official doctor's note on the next class-hour.

**Homework feedback:** LA collects all homework assignments, provides feedback on after the instructor records the submission date, and then returns assignments to students preferably by the next class-hour. However, if in case when you receive homework assignments and the next class-hour is following day, you may return the assignments by the second class-hour after you've received it. LAs are not required to grade small quizzes and chapter tests.

**LA sessions:** All students in your assigned class are required to meet with LA *twice a semester* to converse in Japanese and ask questions on the Japanese grammar as needed. LA needs to keep an LA session *log* for each LA session and submit it to your instructor afterwards. Be careful! If you can't answer student's question with confidence during the session, you must NOT respond to their question with your guess. Be sure to ask your instructor about the question and answer the question for the student later.

**Teaching practice:** LA is required to teach Japanese in their assigned class at least *twice during a semester*: once *in the former* and the other *in the latter* half of the semester. Your instructor will notify you the date of the teaching practice a few weeks in advance so that you can prepare for teaching according to the teacher's instructions. Be sure to receive feedback on your teaching demonstration from your instructor so that you could improve it in the second time.

**Grade**: Pass (P) or No Credit (N)

To receive a grade of P (Pass):

> Must attend class over 90% of class meeting.
> Must attend classes punctually.
> Must be actively involved in class activities.
> Must tutor students outside class-hours, such as LA sessions.
> Must make efforts to speak in Japanese with students.
> Correct student works responsibly.
> Must assist Japanese program's events, e.g., Year End Presentation.
> Submit an excellent paper written about the course.

**Others**: LA may be required to be flexible for some urgent situations, such as teacher's sickness/injury/conference, that may cause a case of being a substitute teacher. Be ready to receive messages from your teacher. Also, LA is expected to work collaboratively with your instructor and students in harmony.

## Appendix 3.2 Peer Tutor Log

Tutoring time: M T W Tr F          Time:          :  ~   :

|  | Tutor | Tutee |
|---|---|---|
| Name |  |  |
| Japanese class and the teacher |  |  |
| Contact info: Email address |  |  |
| Contact info: Phone number |  |  |

1st session

| Date and time : |  |
|---|---|
| Content studied: | Grammar, speaking practice, workbook, other: |
| Comment to instructor: |  |

Note: The above box was printed multiple times so that many sessions could be recorded on the same sheet.

## Appendix 3.3  Certificate of appreciation

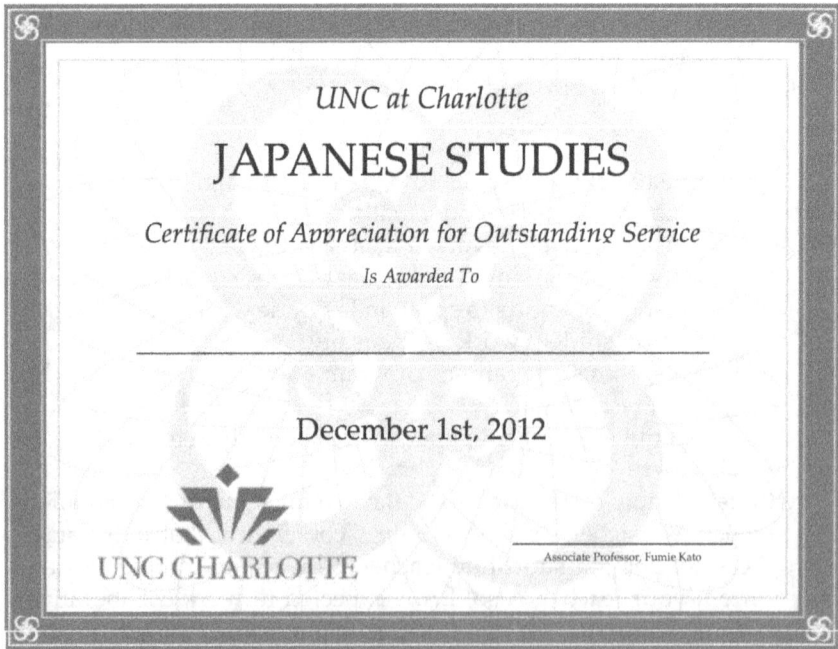

## Notes

1 LAs are, however, required to check homework assignments.
2 Independent courses at UNC Charlotte are considered a method of receiving credit for study or research independent of assignments of any specific course but that are supervised or graded by a faculty member.

# 4 Study abroad opportunities
## Sending and receiving

### 4.1 Introduction

This chapter covers two strategies related to study abroad programs: one can be utilized to increase local communication with native speakers of the TL at learners' home university, and the other deals with enhancing programs that send students abroad to countries where the TL is spoken. While the previous chapters covered strategies to provide learners with opportunities to speak via the Internet or integrating native speakers in the area, this chapter covers how to integrate study abroad into the learning process and describes strategies to foster study abroad programs. It touches on points made in previous chapters, and gives a practical example through the development of study abroad programs and related institutional partnerships that the Japanese program at UNC Charlotte has helped develop in order to garner interest, grow the program and enhance student motivation levels by giving them enjoyable moments related to Japanese language and culture with their fellow students, which ultimately drives participants to study abroad themselves. These strategies are especially important for overcoming both the poverty of opportunity and the poverty of interest problems by helping students to see the TL being used practically in their own local areas and also immersing themselves in the culture of the TL. The chapter introduces case studies of these strategies integrated into the Japanese program at UNC Charlotte, specifically: (1) collaborating with Japanese universities to allow US JFL learners to spend time with Japanese students visiting UNC Charlotte on short-term programs, and (2) enhancing study abroad programs in Japan.

### 4.2 Increasing integrative motivation through collaborative short-term visiting programs

Many language researchers have identified motivation as one of the most influential factors in foreign language acquisition (e.g., Csizér & Dörnyei, 2005; Kato, 2002; MacIntyre & Gardner, 1994; Oxford, 1996; Trembly & Gardner, 1995). However, there are several different types of motivation, which vary not only for individual learners but also depending on the TL. The type of motivation behind learners of minor and major FLs, for example, is bound to be different. While learners of major FLs often study because of external motivation (i.e., they are forced into it, such as in the example of many EFL learners in non-English-speaking countries) or instrumental motivation (desire to accomplish a task, such as taking a certificate and getting a better job) (Dörnyei, 2001b; Gardner & Lambert, 1972), minor foreign language learners are often not pushed into learning the language and are less likely to see the language as important for their immediate lives or future careers. However, minor FL learners can often be motivated through integrative (desire to interact with or belong to another ethnographic group of the learners' TL) and instrumental motivation, which relates specifically to language learning (Gardner & Lambert, 1972). Many researchers (e.g., Dörnyei, 2001b; Gardner & Lambert, 1972; Hernández, 2010; Kato, 2010; Masgoret & Gardner, 2003) have demonstrated that language learners with high integrative motivation focus on developing TL proficiency and seek out opportunities to study. Kato (2007) investigated student motivation among Japanese language learners at UNC Charlotte in 2003, based on a model including eight different kinds of motivation (*Intrinsic, Integrative, Instrumental, Self-Confidence, Anxiety, Motivational Strength, Cooperative,* and *Competitive*), and found that after intrinsic motivation, that is, doing things for the enjoyment of it, integrative motivation was the highest form of motivation among the learners. Based on these results, the Japanese program at UNC Charlotte has employed several teaching strategies fostering students' integrative motivation (Kato, 2010). For example, a collaborative short-term visiting program was developed to enhance students' integrative motivation and solve the poverty of opportunity problem for them. This section focuses on the 2012 and 2013 versions of the collaborative short-term visiting program, which was first implemented in the spring of 2012, and reports how the 2013 version of the program better improved student motivation, as compared to the 2012 version. Finally, advice to instructors who are interested in implementing similar programs is provided.

### 4.2.1 A case study of a collaborative short-term visiting program at UNC Charlotte

The first collaborative short-term visiting program at UNC Charlotte was created by the Japanese program at UNC Charlotte and Sophia University in Japan. Students from these two universities interacted at UNC Charlotte for three weeks. In this program, Japanese students from Sophia University visited UNC Charlotte, giving them the opportunity to be immersed in US society and improve their English language proficiency. During this time, students at UNC Charlotte were also given opportunities to join in activities with the Sophia University students, which we hoped would improve their motivation to learn Japanese.

Although visiting students on short-term programs are immersed in their TL to some degree during their stay, they often have insufficient opportunities to interact with their native counterparts unless specific activities are arranged beforehand because of how limited their time is (Shi, 2011). Furthermore, visiting students' schedules are often occupied by activities, both in and out of the classroom, which are set up by study abroad offices. However, these activities are often conducted with only the students in the short-term program, which limits their ability to make friends and meet native peers with whom they can connect and practice speaking. Therefore, short-term study abroad students often spend their entire trip with only instructors, the caretakers of the program, and people in the community that were part of the planned off-campus social activities (Shi, 2011). This was also the case for students who visited UNC Charlotte from Sophia University before the implementation of our collaborative program.

We thus proposed a collaborative learning program with a "win-win" strategy for the Sophia University short-term visiting program to UNC Charlotte. Because our learners of Japanese at UNC Charlotte have few opportunities to practice Japanese or meet native speakers, and students from Sophia University studying on short-term programs had challenges making friends with local students, the program was created with the aim of fulfilling the needs of both groups of students. The next sections report the outcomes of an exploration of a collaborative short-term visiting program conducted in 2012 and 2013 at UNC Charlotte and look specifically at their influence on the enhancement of learners' motivation to continue learning Japanese and their desire to study abroad in Japan. Data, taken in the form of reflection papers and questionnaires and reported in Kato (2016) was used to help determine how successful the collaborative short-term program was at enhancing students' integrative motivation and solving the poverty of opportunity and interest problems, and how the project influenced participants' Japanese learning afterwards. The program was then revised and carried out again in 2013 based on the formative analysis of the 2012 student data.

### 4.2.2 Preliminary project

#### 4.2.2.1 Email correspondence

A specific course for the project was not offered, so students at UNC Charlotte had to balance the exchange program with their classes and other academic responsibilities, and thus the amount of time that they had to spend with the Japanese students was limited. Participants corresponded with each other via email for one month before the Japanese students arrived in March to overcome this problem. US and Japanese students were paired, and instructed to exchange emails with their partners using their respective TLs throughout the month of February.

*4.2.2.2 Participants*

The participants at UNC Charlotte were learners of Japanese, and the Japanese participants from Sophia University were L1 Japanese EFL learners. At the beginning of the spring semester, instructors at UNC Charlotte explained the collaborative short-term visiting program and recruited 34 US JFL learners who were higher than intermediate level and interested in participating. At the beginning of February, an orientation was held to instruct the US participants about the procedures and requirements of the project. Twenty-nine Sophia University students visited UNC Charlotte in 2012, resulting in 63 total participants.

*4.2.2.3 Program implementation*

The Japanese students arrived in Charlotte on March 1, 2012, to a welcome reception with their email partners, where they met for the first time. During their time in Charlotte, the Japanese students visited several science and technology classes and local businesses in Charlotte, and attended sporting events. UNC Charlotte students could not join their peers for every event due to their regular class schedules and took part in only a few of them. Beyond these planned activities, the US students were expected to try to spend time with the Japanese visiting students according to their own schedules. All participants attended a farewell reception three weeks later.

**4.2.3 Outcomes of the preliminary project**

*4.2.3.1 Participants' perspectives of the short-term visiting program*

A few days after the project's end, UNC Charlotte students submitted reflection papers and responded to a questionnaire ($N = 30$) (see Appendix 4.1). The three most significant questions from the survey were Qs (questions) 3, 5, and 11.

> Q.3 Did you enjoy participating in this collaborative learning program?
> - → 83% agreed
> 
> Q.5 Did this collaborative learning program meet your expectations?
> - →75% agreed
> 
> Q.11 Would you likely participate in this kind of program if offered again?
> - → 93% agreed

The high number of positive responses demonstrated that most of the participants viewed the project favorably. This was further supported by the fact that 26 out of 34 participants later declared Japanese as their Major or Minor, and that over two-thirds of the participants expressed desire to travel to Japan to study in the future. Q.4, which asked why participants volunteered for the program revealed that their primary motivation was to interact with Japanese students, which is indicative of integrative motivation (70%), and the second was to improve their Japanese skills, which is indicative of instrumental motivation (60%). Q.6 asked how often participants corresponded with their partners via email, and revealed that most partners communicated approximately once a week. Q.7 through Q.10 asked about how actively the UNC Charlotte students participated in the activities planned by the university and the social events that the students coordinated independently and showed that although UNC Charlotte students were unable to attend many planned activities, they spent time together outside of the class hours and designated activities, further indicating that they had high levels of integrative motivation. Their social engagements included eating dinner, going shopping, having coffee, ice skating, watching movies, and playing video games.

### 4.2.3.2 Participants' opinions of the short-term visiting program

According to data from the open-ended reflection papers ($N = 21$), analyzed by employing a conceptually clustered matrix analysis (Kato, 2016; Miles & Huberman, 1944), it was found that a majority of the students (71%) were excited to spend time with Japanese students outside of an academic setting, further indicating that they had strong integrative motivation. One student wrote, "We went to Red Robin[1] ... [and we talked] about the differences between American and Japanese women's personalities ... the night was very interesting all in all." All of the participants expressed having enjoyed interacting with the Japanese students, with another writing, "I invited all of the exchange students to my birthday celebration."

The students' responses also indicated that they had high integrative motivation, and that their desires were fulfilled by the program. For example, approximately two thirds of the students expressed excitement, reporting, "I had been crazy excited [about] ... an opportunity to make new friends [from] other countries." Furthermore, two-thirds of the students referred to the pen pal correspondence in a positive manner, noting that they were "very happy," or "excited" when they received responses from their partners, and that they carried out language exchange, saying, "[I] helped him with his English, as he helped [me with my] Japanese." These comments illustrate that corresponding with Japanese students before meeting them was a meaningful experience for the UNC Charlotte students that helped satisfy their integrative motivation by providing authentic interactions with native speakers. Other examples indicating students' high levels of integrative motivation are comments saying how they "loved having a pen pal," "[I] certainly like to participate [in the program] again," "I believe we made a lasting friendship," and "we still wrote even after she returned home."

It was also the first opportunity for many of the UNC Charlotte students to speak with Japanese university students that possess limited English ability due to the fact that most exchange Japanese students at UNC Charlotte have high levels of English proficiency. Students stated, "We all struggled through communication with each other." One participant noted, "this was a great experience to help me to try to explain myself in Japanese." As both groups of students lacked proficient TL abilities, these reflections indicate that participants tried to do their best in order to communicate with one another.

Furthermore, some students mentioned the cultural overlap that manifested in the form of similarities and differences in students' tastes. This demonstrates the value of discovering a foreign culture through direct communication and is evident in the experiences of the US participants in this program by interacting with their Japanese counterparts. This is important because, according to Hernández (2010), there is a positive relationship between motivation, interaction with the culture, and the development of speaking proficiency.

This project also seemed to influence participants' attitudes toward studying abroad in Japan. According to Kato (2016), six students' motivation (29%) to study abroad increased as demonstrated by comments such as, "my desire to visit Japan grew and grew," and the fact that students who wrote such comments later actually did study abroad in Japan. One of these students almost gave up on studying abroad because it was his senior year, but he managed to find the time to attend a short-term summer program. The other student did not initially seem to want to go to Japan, perhaps due to being a Spanish major, but surprisingly attended a study abroad program in Japan for one academic year after participating in this project. These are all good examples of strong integrative motivation, which can be in eventually encouraging students to seek out the opportunity to study abroad (Hernández, 2010).

One-fifth of the comments were negative about the project. The majority of negative comments revolved around difficulty in meeting with the Japanese students during the program. Representative student opinions include, "Unfortunately I did not do as many activities with the Japanese students due to work and school schedule." Although negative, the comment also expressed regretful sentiments, which supports the idea that the UNC Charlotte students participating in this program possess strong integrative motivation. However, these negative comments were also important because they helped identify two problematic issues: lack of transportation and the expense of the events. Two students did not have reliable transportation, that is, a car – a necessity for transportation in the Charlotte region, so it was difficult for them to organize trips with their pen pals. One student said, "A lot of the events did cost quite a lot of money," indicating that economic issues prevented him from participating in more events.

### 4.2.3.3 Formative evaluation

Responses to the three most significant questions, that is, Q.3, Q.5 and Q.12, and the reflections indicate that the program in 2012 was satisfactory, but there were areas that could be improved. The second project was implemented in 2013 and built upon this critical feedback in order to address the lacking areas.

The 2013 program implemented new procedures by creating small correspondence groups rather than pairs in order to address the problems indicated by the quantitative and qualitative analyses. Two other issues were also considered when organizing groups for 2013: student access to transportation and spring break occurring during the program. Countermeasures for these problems were to ensure that at least one student who owns a car was included in each group, and creating a balance of students who did and did not plan to leave Charlotte over spring break.

### **4.2.4 Revised project**

### 4.2.4.1 Participants

The same methods for recruitment were utilized as in 2012, resulting in 57 participants (34 US and 23 Japanese students) in the 2013 collaborative short-term visiting program. Eleven groups were formed based on student availability and transportation. All students were required to exchange emails within their groups throughout February. After the program, all US students responded to the same questionnaires made for the project in 2012 and were required to submit a reflection paper after the program.

### **4.2.5 Comparison of the program over two years**

### 4.2.5.1 Participants' perspectives of the short-term visiting program

Student survey responses ($N = 30$) were analyzed, and the responses to the three most significant questions, that is, Q.3, Q.5 and Q.11, given by UNC Charlotte students for the two years were compared. No significant differences were found between 2012 and 2013 responses for Q.3 and Q.11, but one was observed for Q.5 ($\chi^2$ (2, $N = 64$) = 0.074, $p < .01$) (Kato, 2016). This means that more students had their expectations fulfilled in 2013 than in 2012.

Other survey results suggested that students in 2013 were more actively engaged than those in 2012. For example, responses to Q.6 indicated that participants in 2013 corresponded much more frequently than the students in 2012, which might have stimulated their integrative motivation more than in 2012. Furthermore, a comparison of Q.7 through Q.10, which asked participants about which activities they joined, suggested that participants in 2013 attended the events more actively, spent much more time with their native speaking peers outside of the events, met the Japanese students more frequently, and took part in other social activities such as bowling, playing video games, and visiting the houses of their pen pals (Kato, 2016).

*4.2.5.2 Participants' opinions of the short-term visiting program*

Twenty-nine reflection papers (out of 34) were collected in 2013 and analyzed through the same procedures as in 2012.

Only two opinions in the student reflections were written about significantly more in 2013 than in 2012. The first regarded how well they were able to make friends, with more positive comments about their friendships appearing in 2013 ($\chi^2 = .0354, p < .05$). Because they were successful in forming friendships during this short period, many participants in 2013 were very sad when they attended the farewell party. One of the positive comments from the reflection papers included a student who was, "sad to say 'Goodbye'," and seven students (24%) expressed sadness, writing comment such as, "The group of Sophia girls ... nearly shed tears as we said our goodbyes." The second revolved around motivation to study abroad. Eleven students (38%) wrote that they intended to visit the Japanese students in Japan and that they had concrete arrangements to go, a significant improvement over the previous year ($\chi^2 = .0115, p < .05$), and they gave comment such as, "XX gave me his address in Tokyo ... I need to go and see him ... I could stay at his house and we would ride motorcycles together." These results suggested that the project in 2013 enhanced US students' motivation to travel to see their friends in Japan, indicating an increase in integrative motivation (Hernández, 2010).

Students in 2013 gave three kinds of suggestions: (1) posting the event schedule sooner, (2) making the program longer, and (3) making pairs instead of groups. Nine students (31%) stated that they could have attended more events if they had received the program agenda in advance, because "[We could have been] able to schedule our jobs." Five students (17%) requested that the program be longer than three weeks, noting, "Three weeks seemed like five days," whereas there were no students in 2012 that commented on the length of the program. These comments indicate how strong the desire of participants in 2013 was to spend time with the Japanese students and demonstrate the strength of their integrative motivation, manifested in an insistent desire to get to know their peers. While some students in 2013 suggested pairs rather than groups, perhaps due to a desire to make more personal connections, no students in 2013 mentioned a lack of transportation, indicating that creating groups was an effective way to solve this problem, an improvement over the 2012 program.

### 4.2.6 Discussion and conclusions from the data

The results of the data, as reported here and in Kato (2016) surrounding the collaborative short-term visiting program showed that many students already possessed strong integrative motivation and that it was further enhanced by bringing them together with Japanese students for a three-week period in their home country. This outcome is in line with Norris-Holt (2001) who saw students' motivation elevated after having sessions with a TL group.

In terms of how well the project met the demands of the students' integrative motivation, most of the participants indicated that the project fulfilled their expectations, which helped to push their integrative motivation further. For example, the vast majority stated that they would like to participate in the project again if it were to be offered in future. Overall, the proactive participation from participants and their comments on their interactions indicate that the poverty of opportunity was lessened, and the positive comments and opinions from participants suggest that poverty of interest problem was also diminished.

The project was also found to have improved student motivation levels to learn Japanese continuously, and that their integrative motivation was strengthened, specifically in terms of their motivation toward studying abroad in Japan. This is reflected in the fact that six students (25%) in 2012 wrote about their desire to study abroad in the future, and in 2013, 12 students (41%) were looking forward to meeting their Japanese friends again in Japan. Furthermore, these indications seemed to bear out in the future when considering student participation numbers in Japanese study abroad programs at UNC Charlotte from 2003 to 2014.

Twenty participants from the collaborative short-term visiting program in 2012 and 2013 are included in the Table 4.1. Student participation rates rose considerably from 2012 (after the program) and although it cannot be determined if participation in the program was the only factor associated with this rise, the increase from 2012 indicates that this program likely at least influenced it.

The collaborative short-term visiting program provided students with an opportunity to socialize with native Japanese students and to act on their integrative motivation locally. Furthermore, their heightened integrative motivation can be associated with an increase in desire to study abroad in Japan. For these reasons, I consider such programs to be invaluable for

Table 4.1 Study abroad student participation numbers in the Japanese program at UNC Charlotte

| Academic year | '03 | '04 | '05 | '06 | '07 | '08 | '09 | '10 | '11 | '12 | '13 | '14 |
|---|---|---|---|---|---|---|---|---|---|---|---|---|
| Long-term | 10 | 4 | 11 | 11 | 14 | 13 | 11 | 12 | 16 | 22 | 19 | 21 |
| Short-term | 0 | 0 | 0 | 0 | 0 | 1 | 0 | 2 | 0 | 2 | 1 | 3 |
| **Total** | **10** | **4** | **11** | **11** | **14** | **14** | **11** | **14** | **16** | **24** | **20** | **24** |
| Registered students ($n$) | 264 | 350 | 393 | 427 | 559 | 664 | 691 | 796 | 852 | 841 | 790 | 835 |
| Participating students (%) | 3.8 | 1.1 | 2.8 | 2.6 | 2.5 | 2.1 | 1.6 | 1.8 | 1.9 | 2.9 | 2.5 | 2.9 |

Note: '03 indicates the year 2003.

solving the poverty of opportunity and poverty of interest problems for minor FL learners, such as the Japanese learners at UNC Charlotte.

### 4.2.7 Advice for creating and conducting collaborative short-term visiting programs

Instructors of minor or major FLs who want to increase the integrative motivation of their students while providing them opportunities to speak with native speakers should consider creating similar collaborative short-term visiting programs. While this of course requires that there are visitors from elsewhere who speak the learners' TL, such programs are far more common than one might think. For example, even if there is not a group of students who will come for a short-term visit, small groups of researchers or visiting professors often spend time at foreign universities. There might even be tourist groups or temporary workers who come to nearby businesses. By considering all of these possibilities, it increases the likelihood that you can find collaborators, which is especially important for teachers of minor FLs. If there are no such programs currently in or around the community, it might even be plausible for one to contact teachers at foreign universities who might then consider bringing a group of students. Such an arrangement will be mutually beneficial for everyone involved. However, regardless of how collaborators are recruited, there are several points that instructors who would like to create a similar collaborative short-term visiting program should consider.

First, it is best to select an appropriate number of participants. While instructors may want to include all of their students, too much of an imbalance in participants and collaborators can dilute the positive effects that such a program can offer to students. When trying to decide which students to include, my recommendation is to look at their language level. As much as possible, I suggest selecting participants with at least an intermediate level who have learned their TL for at least a year. In the case of the program at UNC Charlotte, elementary level students had only studied Japanese for either less than one month or less than four months when the collaborative short-term visiting program started because it was scheduled for February. It would have been difficult for them to conduct email exchange or communicate in their TL. Of course, if there is enough room in the program, even elementary level learners can have an enjoyable experience talking with the visitors in their mother tongue, learn culture through the visitors, and this may also influence their motivation, helping them to feel that the TL is tangible and of importance. This could in turn motivate them to keep learning their TL further.

Second, although some students may prefer pair-work when doing email exchanging tasks, I recommend making this a group activity because this helps overcome imbalances in participation. Furthermore, making groups with four to five students can help with a number of problems that might occur during the visit such as that of transportation, participation during spring break, and email exchange, as outlined in the case study.

Furthermore, instructors should consult university administration before creating such a program. If the visitors are students, as in the case of UNC Charlotte, there is often a particular office that is responsible for incoming study abroad students and they set up the contract between host and overseas educational institutions. This is still important if dealing with visiting researchers or other groups, such as local businesses, as the university will likely have some role or responsibility if an official university-supported program is created. However, although other university faculty may help to establish any contracts and agreements, please be aware that the responsibility for advertising and recruiting participants will generally fall on the instructor.

Finally, if recruiting partner institutions from overseas, the most important factor to consider for a collaborative short-term visiting program is the timeframe. Instructors should try to schedule programs for times that are convenient not only for collaborative partners, but also for their own students so as to increase the duration and frequency that visitors and students can interact. However, there are often a number of different restrictions on both groups, and sometimes instructors must simply aim for a comfortable middle ground. In the case study, it was scheduled for February because most Japanese universities finish their fall semester in February and have a spring break in March. However, although this timing is convenient for Japanese university students, it is in the middle of the spring semester at most US universities, which created some problems for the UNC Charlotte students. This ultimately resulted in time constraints on interactions between students, but as the Japanese university students are the ones paying to come to the United States, there is little that I could do about this. While finding times when all of the students are on break, such as the beginning of August, are best, when it is not possible, instructors should strive to help their students schedule time, transportation and funds to spend as much time as possible with the visitors.

## 4.3 The importance of studying abroad opportunity and institutional partnerships

Promoting study abroad programs is important to create human resources who have intricate knowledge of cross-cultural understanding, interpersonal communication skills and global perspectives, all of which are necessary in international or multinational companies. In this way, it is a kind of a grassroots activity that is very important for the future relationships of any two countries. However, it is also critical for raising TL skills, as mentioned throughout this book, and encouraging the number of students that will enter one's own institution. Raising the number of incoming foreign students will also help instructors to create a number of innovative and immersive opportunities for students while studying a minor FL in their own home country. A vast expanse of literature suggests that one of the best ways to help students of minor FLs overcome the poverty of opportunity and poverty of interest problems is to have them study abroad where the TL is primarily used (e.g., Conteras Jr., 2015; Jon, Shin, & Fry, 2018; Tajes & Ortiz, 2010). If students can spend time living where the TL is used as a lingua franca, they will not only have many opportunities to interact with the language, solving the poverty of opportunity, but they will have to use the language practically in their day to day lives, overcoming the poverty of interest. Therefore, one of the core missions of the Japanese program at UNC Charlotte is to send as many of our students as possible to study in Japan, and many of my efforts during my tenure there have been focused on increasing the number of students who go. To this end, new study abroad programs and partnerships have been created with several different universities in Japan. However, creating and maintaining study abroad programs is not only the job of study abroad offices, but also the instructors of FLs who must garner interest in their students. This is particularly true for minor FLs where interest may decrease. To this end, educators must also be vigilant to increase the number of exchange partner universities and ensure that enough students are going in both directions. This section details the effectiveness and necessity of study abroad experience as pointed out in previous research, and then describes procedures to enhance learners' willingness to study abroad, including several tricks and tips which the Japanese program at UNC Charlotte has employed.

### 4.3.1 Effectiveness and necessity of studying abroad

Study abroad programs have been an integral part of the curriculum of higher education since 1875 (DiMaggio, 2016). Since then, many studies have reported that they have an overall positive impact on educational outcomes such as enhanced knowledge and understanding of the participants' host and home countries (Tajes & Ortiz, 2010), personal growth (Contreras Jr., 2015), global perspective (Contreras Jr., 2015; Jon et al., 2018; Paige, Fry, Stallman, Josic, & Jon, 2009; Tajes & Ortiz, 2010), cross-cultural understanding/communication (Contreras Jr., 2015; Yang, 2005), interpersonal skills and confidence (Yang, 2005), academic gains (Jon et al., 2018; Contreras Jr., 2015; Niser, 2010; Paige et al., 2009), specifically TL acquisition (Jon et al., 2018; Tajes & Ortiz, 2010), and increased retention of studying (DiMaggio, 2016).

Students who study abroad also become more competitive in the job market (Jon et al., 2018) because they have generally gained skills that are attractive to employers (Niser, 2010). According to Niser (2010), there is "a relation between employability and attending a study abroad program because of the growing need for understanding the world economically, politically, culturally, and socially" (p. 50). Employers thus tend to seek job candidates with international study experiences (Yang, 2005). Study abroad participants develop career identities by living in a different environment and having diverse experiences (Jon et al., 2018), which sometimes influences participants to change their educational and career plans (Jon et al., 2018; Paige et al., 2009; Tajes & Ortiz, 2010), as evidenced by the fact that students who study abroad have a strong tendency to seek international careers or jobs at multinational companies (Jon et al., 2018).

However, there are currently not enough US students who have participated in study abroad programs to fill the requirements of international businesses. The National Association of Foreign Student Affairs (NAFSA, an association of international educators), reported in 2014 that almost 40% of companies could not find enough internationally competent personnel, and Tajes and Ortiz (2010) pointed out that there are "severe national deficiencies such as the absence of qualified personnel for filling national security positions or playing key roles in fostering international relations and policy making" (p. 18). According to NAFSA's report during 2016–2017, the number of US students studying abroad grew 2.3% which represented 1.6% of all US students and 10% of US graduate of higher education in the USA. Thus, higher education institutions in the United States still need to emphasize on the gains in "intercultural communication, foreign language skills and international experience" that can be gained from study abroad and furthermore, "… additional international business education programs will need to be developed, particularly programs with a focus on Asia" (Daniel, Xie, & Kedia, 2014, p. 1). Increasing study abroad is also important to internationalize US campuses and help students succeed in a world increasing in global interconnections (Dvorak, Christiansen, Fischer, & Underhill, 2011).

UNC Charlotte stresses the importance of diversity and strives to increase global literacy, with one of its core mission statements being to provide "an accessible and affordable quality education that equips students with intellectual and professional skills, ethical principles, and an international perspective." Therefore, it strongly encourages students to study abroad before graduating. The Japanese program has also recognized the necessity of sending its students' abroad, and has developed several tactics to increase the number of participants and exchange partner universities, as detailed in the next section.

### 4.3.2 Study abroad programs in the Japanese program

Students in the Japanese program at UNC Charlotte are eligible to study abroad after they have finished taking the first three semesters (180 regular class-hours) of Japanese language courses, that is, finished taking the intermediate I course. During these three semesters, students learn reading, writing, listening and speaking as well as Japanese grammar, culture and lifestyle. Students who have learned Japanese for at least three semesters can communicate in Japanese, but only on a very basic level. This is truly the best time for them to be immersed in Japanese, because they have already mastered the grammar and vocabulary required for basic communication, but have not yet developed communicative skills to a practical level, particularly speaking and listening skills, which are quite difficult to attain in a minor FL learning environment. After learning the basics, living in a society that speaks the TL can help minor FL learners gain communicative abilities more easily than when living in their home country. For Japanese students at UNC Charlotte, this means that they can use the Japanese knowledge that they learned in the previous three/four semesters and then progress their Japanese language proficiencies effectively, internalizing the explicit knowledge that they learned in their classes. Learners who study abroad without any prior knowledge of the TL often end up learning only basic skills, which they can obtain without an immersive environment. Therefore, sending students who have already mastered the basic level courses allows them to make the most of their study abroad experience.

In consideration of the aforementioned language study factors and students' schedules, the most appropriate time for most UNC Charlotte students, and presumably most at other US universities, to study abroad is in their third year. Students in their third year have often studied their TL for three or four semesters, and can then be immersed in the TL society during their junior year. This then leaves students with one academic year to finish their degrees for graduation when they return. Since their TL proficiency level will have presumably improved significantly after one-year of immersion, they can use the knowledge and skills that they acquired abroad to enjoy learning in advanced level courses. In the Japanese program at UNC Charlotte, for example, several advanced classes are offered including translation classes for undergraduate and graduate translation certificates, advanced oral communication, advanced spoken business Japanese, introductory research project, JLPT Prep, senior seminar, inter-collaborative peer learning, and an honors research course. Students who declare Japanese as their major are required to take four of these advanced courses, so these courses are specifically offered to them and the difficulty level is high. Although it can be extremely challenging for the students, returnees from Japan generally enjoy these advanced level classes that help them to maintain and further develop their Japanese language proficiencies. This is another reason why as many of my students as possible are strongly recommended to study abroad in Japan.

Students are also recommended to study abroad for a full academic year when possible. Most UNC Charlotte students who study abroad in Japan experience severe culture shock at first, and it generally takes them one or two months to overcome it and to get used to life in Japan. Furthermore, their Japanese language classes are generally taught entirely in Japanese because they take classes together with other study abroad students who have a wide variety of first languages, making Japanese the lingua franca. This is often shocking and a bit difficult for UNC Charlotte students who are used to learning Japanese with English as the instructional language. It generally takes them one or two months to get used to this as well. Therefore, most UNC Charlotte students spend the first semester after they arrive in Japan coping with their new life and studying style. Students who study abroad for a full academic year generally enjoy their lives in the second semester, spend fruitful time and enjoy Japan itself by making Japanese friends, participating in student organizations, taking trips or working part-time jobs introduced by their host universities. For this reason, students at UNC Charlotte often tell me that they cry twice when studying abroad: once just after arriving in Japan because of the huge differences in lifestyle, and once more just before leaving Japan because they don't want to leave the environment with which they have familiarized themselves and have fallen in love with.

When UNC Charlotte students return from studying abroad in Japan, they often experience reverse culture shock due to the huge differences in customs and life styles. It is at this point that they realize how much knowledge they acquired through their study abroad experience and how much they have changed. This is not uncommon for study abroad returnees, with several studies mentioning that the experience frequently causes participants to change directions in their studies and career preferences (e.g., Jon et al., 2018; Paige et al., 2009; Tajes & Ortiz, 2010). UNC Charlotte returnees often recall their days and lives in Japan fondly, and so recently, the number of students who would like to go back to Japan for work after graduation has been gradually increasing, which is congruent with the findings of works such as Jon et al. (2018). These students are valuable human resources who can bridge the gap between the United States and Japan because they know the advantages and disadvantages, cultures, customs and lifestyles of both countries. Every year meeting a new group of returnees reminds me that the work we are doing is significant and meaningful, causing me to redouble my efforts to send students each year. Surely, without sending students abroad, minor FL teachers alone cannot create such human resources. This is the biggest reason why study abroad programs are strongly promoted to all of JFL students at UNC Charlotte.

### 4.3.3 Strategies for recruiting students to study abroad

Recently, there has been a steady increase of freshmen who intend to pursue a Japanese BA degree at UNC Charlotte and plan to study abroad in Japan. However, the majority of students do not know about the Japanese program in detail or the study abroad opportunities. Such students often simply take Japanese language courses on their friends' recommendations or due to an interest in Japanese anime, video games or culture. Therefore, the faculty needs to explain the Japanese BA degree and study abroad programs to them as soon as they start taking elementary level courses. Since many students in the Japanese program choose to study abroad after taking three or four semesters of Japanese, instructors need to start explaining the study abroad programs in detail in at least their second semester because it often takes about one semester to prepare the study abroad application, and students are required to submit it six months prior to their departure. As the process can be quite daunting, it is necessary to give counseling and guidance to students who intend to study abroad to ensure that they can successfully submit the application. This sort of assistance is particularly important for students who are still undecided about going. Though they may feel that there is plenty of time, they in fact must hurry because they must also complete the appropriate paperwork. Therefore, I have developed a system of strategies and procedures to introduce and motivate students to participate in study abroad programs at UNC Charlotte.

First, each instructor in the Japanese program explains the study abroad programs in their own classes, especially elementary- and intermediate-level Japanese classes. At this stage, it is the first time for many students to hear about the study abroad programs in Japan, and they often do not imagine that they themselves will actually go. As many students are unsure about studying abroad, it is vital for instructors to follow up with eligible students and speak to each one individually, face to face, to gauge their intention to study abroad and recommend an appropriate program to them. If students are unwelcoming of the idea, instructors are encouraged to ask why, as there are times when the faculty can help support them (e.g., scholarships to help with financial worries, special seminars to alleviate concerns about adaptability). However, instructors do not push if students have unavoidable reasons such as their GPA not being good enough or their other major being too busy. Furthermore, although freshman and sophomore students enrolled in elementary levels are able to participate in study abroad programs, it is unfortunately, too late for junior and senior students enrolled in elementary levels to go to Japan for even one semester because study abroad returnees have to stay for at least one final semester at UNC Charlotte before their graduation.

Another way to garner interest in studying abroad is by holding a "Study Abroad Report" every fall semester. At UNC Charlotte, returnees from studying abroad give presentations about their lives and experiences in Japan. It is an opportunity for returnees to report and talk about their fantastical, unusual, precious, enjoyable or humorous experiences in Japan, and also an opportunity for students who are interested in studying abroad to hear what it is really like. As this event is held one or two months after students have returned from studying abroad, their memories and experiences are still fresh in their minds, and they are generally pleased to reminisce and share their episodes with other returnees and potential study abroad candidates. Students form groups with others who attended the same Japanese host university and each talks for seven to eight minutes, allowing three minutes for questions and answers. The presenters are required to talk about information on scholarships, dormitories, the cost of living, student organizations, Japanese courses (including the textbooks that they used), and can also choose to regale the listeners with humorous anecdotes or stories about what they enjoyed abroad. Episodes, especially experiences of failure, become excellent advice for future study abroad students. For example, one student parked her bicycle illegally and it was impounded quite far from where she was, so she had to walk very far to retrieve it and pay a fine at the police box. One student reported that he got lost on his way back to his dormitory and had to solve the problem himself, which forced him to seek out the help of many Japanese people. Future study abroad students listen to these experiences and look forward to their own failures, as they often become excellent learning experiences. Having such experiences is incredibly valuable for people while they are still young because during this time their futures are still malleable and so studying abroad can completely change their lives afterwards (Jon et al., 2018; Paige et al., 2009; Tajes & Ortiz, 2010).

This event also helps instructors learn about returnees' experiences in Japan and get information on actual programs held at our exchange partner universities. Furthermore, it affords returnees an opportunity to share their experiences, and allows potential students to understand what study abroad programs are like. Their reports have been extremely beneficial and informative, as it helps them to plan advanced classes for returnees, and if student experiences were not as expected, it can help instructors when recommending programs to other students in the future, or can be a clue that they need to renegotiate with or make different requests of exchange partner universities.

The UNC Charlotte Office of Education Abroad (henceforth "OEA") also creates opportunities for returnees to share their experiences with potential study abroad students. They hold a "Study Abroad Fair" every semester, open to all UNC Charlotte students. Volunteers who participated in study abroad programs the previous year are recruited to talk about their experiences to students who are interested in studying abroad in their future. These information exchange sessions help study abroad candidates decide which program they would like to attend and increase their motivation to go through the complex procedures required.

Once students have decided to study abroad, their attitudes generally change dramatically. They become much more motivated to learn Japanese, and must be more proactive in their studies, as there are many things to do in preparation such as meeting with OEA staff members, obtaining recommendation letters from professors, completing application forms, participating in OEA orientations, and applying for a passport and visa. To help support these students, a predeparture orientation is held for students studying abroad the following semester. The goals of the orientation are to: introduce the students going abroad to each other so that they will know who will go to the same university and who might live close by in case of emergency, explain what they are required to do while studying abroad, and recommend things to do in Japan, for example, take the JLPT (Japanese language proficiency test), join a student organization, make many friends, participate in community activities, and actively work to enjoy their lives abroad. Students in the Japanese program generally prepare to leave the United States during the summer holiday and then depart to Japan in the fall. It is the time for all of the study abroad students' dream to come true!

## Appendix 4.1 Questionnaire for short-term visiting program (questions only)

1. Declared Japanese:     1) Major     2) Minor     3) Not yet

2. Japanese Study Abroad Program:
   1) Want to go
   2) Went: Length:     1) One year     2) One semester
   3) A few weeks
   3) Not interested

3. I enjoyed participating in this short-term visiting program:
   1) Strongly agree     2) Agree     3) Neutral     4) Disagree
   5) Strongly disagree

4. Why did you participate in this short-term visiting program?
   1) Meet Japanese     2) Improve my Japanese skills
   3) Get some extra points
   4) Others:_____

5   Did this short-term visiting program meet your expectations?
    1) Yes        2) No

6   How many times did you correspond (email, Facebook, IM) before your pen pal arrived in Charlotte?
    1) Once    2) Twice    3) Three times    4) Four times
    5) Five times (If more than five times, please write the number)

7   How many program-organized events did you attend?
    1) Once    2) Twice    3) Three times    4) Four times
    5) Five times (If more than five times, please write the number)_____
    Please, specify the events:_____

8   Did you spend time with the Japanese participants outside of events?
    1) Yes        2) No

9   If yes, how many times did you meet with the Japanese participants?
    1) Once    2) Twice    3) Three times    4) Four times
    5) Five times (If more than five times, please write the number)

10  If yes, what did you do with the Japanese participants? Circle the appropriate answer and indicate in the brackets the number of times you did each of the activities
    1) Went shopping (    )          2) Saw a movie (    )
    3) Ate dinner out (    )         4) Went sightseeing (    )
    5) Went for coffee/snacks        6) Other activities (please specify):

11  Would you likely participate in this kind of program if offered again?
    1) Yes        2) No

12  Please write any additional comments you may wish to add about your participation in the "Short-Term Visiting Program"

## Note

1  A popular American restaurant in the area.

# 5 Growing interest through extracurricular activities

## 5.1 Introduction

Chapter 5 describes two representative extracurricular activities and efforts that help garner interest in learning Japanese at UNC Charlotte in order to enhance student motivation levels, and grow the program by giving students enjoyable moments related to Japanese language and culture. The main focus of this chapter will be placed on the following two tactics: (1) "Year-End Presentations," in which all of the Japanese language classes get together at the end of each year; and (2) a "Speech Contest," which provides the precious experience of giving a speech in Japanese in front of an audience. These activities help by not only raising students' enthusiasm through practically utilizing their Japanese language abilities, but also by fostering lower-level learners' interest toward Japanese learning through the efforts of senior students and their performances.

## 5.2 Examples of events and efforts that help with interest in Japanese at UNC Charlotte

The events described in this section were created and are conducted by the Japanese program at UNC Charlotte. The faculty in the Japanese program is mindful of them all and uses them to their advantage to recruit students, help to eliminate the poverty of interest and poverty of opportunity problems, and decrease attrition rates. While these activities are described in the lens of studying Japanese at UNC Charlotte, they are easily adaptable to other minor FLs. While they may need to be modified depending on the learning institution, some version of these activities can help drive interest in a similar way, helping with the poverty of interest problem.

### 5.2.1 Year-end presentations

In the spring semester of 2004, I taught a fourth semester Japanese course (intermediate II) in which 12 students were enrolled. I planned for them to perform a Japanese folk tale skit as part of their class activities. They had to present it at the end of the semester as part of their final grade. The aims of this activity were to strengthen the bonds amongst classmates through group work, to make unique memories with their classmates, and prepare them to proceed to upper courses. I wanted students to enjoy the task while working with their fellow students, and I assisted as much as possible.

Students worked in groups to write scripts for one folk tale in Japanese, memorize the lines, and perform it as a skit. During the first trial, students selected Japanese folk tales such as "Urashima Taro," "Monkey and Jizo," or "Peach Boy," all of which were included as reading materials in their textbooks. Although the students were familiar with the stories from their lessons and had already acquired quite a lot of Japanese grammar, they did not have any experience in translating English into Japanese, so I, as their instructor, helped them to translate the lines into Japanese.

I announced the project to my students directly after the end of the first half of the spring semester. This left them with one and a half months to complete the task by the end of the semester. They were instructed to do the following four tasks: (1) divide themselves into three groups, (2) select a group leader, (3) assign roles in their skits, and (4) write the lines of their skit in English. It took a few weeks for them to finish these tasks because only a small portion of the class-hours was designated to this project. As soon as students received their revised Japanese scripts, they began practicing reading and memorizing them, as well as preparing the necessary props for their skits. As they did not have enough time to finish all of these tasks during the class-hours, they had to practice on their own time and rehearse outside of the class-hours as well. On the last day of the semester, all of the students in my class performed their skits to celebrate their accomplishments and successful study that semester.

On the day of the presentation, after all of the performances were finished, students were required to write comments on each play, such as the good points or what could be improved upon. Students praised their classmates, writing things such as, "good acting, very good story, good props, well planned out, good pronunciation of Japanese." However, they also offered advice for the future, such as one student who pointed out, "memorize & get props ready, practice, didn't talk a lot, all actors need to pay attention to the story, need props, need to learn order of lines." From this activity, I realized that students learned several important things through their performances and related peer interactions.

I reported this activity as one of my teaching strategies to enhance students' motivation levels to other Japanese teaching staff members, and they agreed that it could be an effective approach to foster students' willingness to learn, and some of them integrated similar skits into their own classes the following semester. In the spring semester of 2006, on the basis of our collective experiences, all instructors agreed to have their classes conduct skits in an intra-program event carried out by the Japanese

*Table 5.1* Semester-end presentations program

| Time | Item | Group |
|---|---|---|
| 1:00–1:55 | Preparation | |
| 2:00–2:20 | 1. Taiko performance | Kuroshio Taiko team |
| 2:25–2:30 | 2. Opening word, Agenda, Announcement | Nihon Club |
| 2:30–2:35 | 3. Song "IROHANIHOHETO" | 1201 elementary 1 |
| 2:35–2:40 | 4. Song "Japanese verb song" | 1202 elementary 2 |
| 2:40–2:55 | 5. Skit "Godzilla attacks 1201" | 1201 elementary 1 |
| 2:55–3:00 | 6. Song "What a Wonderful World" | 1202 elementary 2 |
| 3:00–3:05 | 7. Presentation "Kabuki Theater" | 1202 elementary 2 |
| 3:05–3:10 | 8. Presentation "Nihon-To (Japanese Sword)" | 1202 elementary 2 |
| 3:10–3:30 | 9. Jyanken game | 3202 u-intermediate 2 |
| 3:30–3:45 | 10. Skit "Japanese cooking show" | 2201 intermediate 1 |
| 3:45–3:55 | 11. Presentation "Japanese cooking" | 1202 elementary 2 |
| 3:55–4:10 | 12. Skit "Black Hair" | 2202 intermediate 2 |
| 4:10–4:20 | 13. Presentation "Smith Academy volunteer" | 3800 independent |
| 4:20–4:35 | 14. Skit "Hekkoki yomesan" | 3201 u-intermediate 1 |
| 4:35–4:45 | 15. Presentation "Web Japanese reading tool" | 3800 independent |
| 4:45–4:55 | 16. Traditional Japanese Dance: Soran Bushi | Nihon Club* |
| 4:55–5:00 | Closing ceremony, Prize Raffle | Coordinator |
| –6:00 | Clean up | |

Note: * "Nihon Club" is a student organization that supports students learning Japanese.

program at the end of the semester and "Semester-End Presentations" started to be integrated in the Japanese program. It was held between 2:00 and 5:00 PM on the final Saturday of the spring semester. Regrettably, there is no record of the number of the participants, but the program for that day has been repeated as Table 5.1.

As shown in Table 5.1, one of the aims of this activity is to provide learners with an experience to participate and perform in Japanese on stage in front of an audience. One great challenge in 2006 was that students in my elementary I class also wanted to perform a skit, but that class is for students who have no prior knowledge of Japanese and are learning it for the first time that semester. Since their level was very low and they did not know any Japanese folk tales, students created a story for the event. They reviewed what they had learned that semester and decided on the title, "Godzilla attacks 1201 (elementary I class)" (the fifth performance in Table 5.1). All of the students had to recite at least one line in Japanese and they were required to memorize their own lines. It was a really simple slapstick comedy, but the students enjoyed it profusely and could use the Japanese that they had learned in the class in context. The student who played the role of Godzilla even made a stuffed tale and a mane. The students mentioned that they were excited by the skit, and I believe the pleasure of achieving a goal with their classmates became a great motivator for them to progress to the next level of Japanese and continue studying.

By having students from all levels participate in the event together and also inviting other groups, such as the Nihon Club and Taiko Team to join, students were able to have a widely positive and motivating experience. Not only could they use the Japanese that they had learned in their class and present their skits to others, they could also see the advanced levels of upperclassmen and were hopefully motivated to become as proficient as the more advanced students. Furthermore, the presentations of cultural points, such as Japanese swords, dances and taiko drums hopefully introduced these to interested students who could then participate in many of the related clubs and activities in the future.

The semester-end presentations in the spring semester of 2006 were so successful, that the Japanese program began to hold them every semester, albeit with minor improvements each time. For example, in the following fall semester of 2006, an instructor created a flyer to invite all students to participate in the event. Although participation was part of Japanese classes, it was decided that students should not be forced to participate in it, specifically because it was held outside of class-hours, which meant that some students were unavailable due to part-time jobs or other obligations. The instructors decided to give one extra point to the students who performed on stage as an incentive to participate. Furthermore, as the event was held on a Saturday, students who attended the event as audience members could make up an in-class absence. This means that student could receive two extra points (2/100) by performing, an attractive incentive for students who needed more points to get a better grade. In the fall of 2007, one instructor created a program using PowerPoint, which was shown in the theater on the day of the event. It was the first time to collect information on the number of the students who participated in the event. In total 74 participants enjoyed the semester-end presentations in 2007. After two years, the semester-end presentations received financial support from the Office of International Programs in the form of a $50 stipend per semester. Using the funds, we began to serve snacks, drinks and give presents ($10 gift cards) to two winners of a game played at the end of the presentations, which was designed to make the audience want to stay until the end of the program. From 2009, the number of participants increased to over 100, with 109 audience members in the fall of 2009, 120 in the spring of 2010, and 143 in the fall 2010. This event has become one of the biggest undertakings of the Japanese program.

The students' enhanced motivation could be seen each year in the sheer amount of effort that they put into their skits and presentations. For example, my intermediate I class (third semester) performed a Star Wars skit and created an intricate PowerPoint with music from the movie to go along with it as well as genuine costumes. Needless to say, they also worked hard to remember their lines and improved their Japanese skills while having a memorable and enjoyable experience. Every year I am deeply impressed with all of our students who always try their best.

With the implementation of LAs (see Chapter 4) in each class, the burden on instructors was lessened. Japanese university students who took the roles of LAs were given roles in their classes' skits, and they practiced them together with their classmates. US learners said lines in Japanese, whereas Japanese students would say lines in English and students were considerate to help each other practice their target languages. Before the implementation of LAs, instructors needed to help their students with every aspect of their skits, but once LAs began being assigned to each class, instructors asked LAs to practice with their classmates and help them create the skits. All LAs were pleased to help their classmates and perform together with them. Therefore, instructors could use the time to supervise and work on the preparation of the program itself.

The Japanese program held semester-end presentations at the end of every semester for several years until this biannual event became a once a year event. The Japanese program was also tasked with organizing a Japanese speech contest (see the following section) every semester, and unfortunately, the burden of doing both of these events every semester became too much for both instructors and students. In 2010, the program then decided to hold the speech contest at the beginning of the spring semester, and presentations at the end of the fall semester, at which time the name of the event was changed to "Year-End Presentations." Students who were very excited about semester-end presentations were disappointed to hear this, but were consoled that they could still participate in the event once per year. In 2014, the year-end presentations were moved to Friday afternoons instead of Saturdays in order to attract as many participants as possible. Some students and faculty members found it inconvenient to come to the university on the weekend, but since language classes are held on Fridays, it was thought that holding the event on Fridays wouldn't create any additional burden. Due to this arrangement, a total of 190 participants enjoyed the presentations in 2014. At that time, the chair of the department and professors from the Office of International Programs were also invited to the event and gave a few words of encouragement to the students. By creating an intra-program collaborative event that includes all of the students studying Japanese, the program was thus able to receive university-wide recognition, and the students gained an enjoyable activity that they could participate in every year.

### 5.2.2 UNC Charlotte Japanese speech contest

A speech contest, called the UNC Charlotte Japanese Speech Contest (henceforth, "speech contest"), has been held every semester from 2007 until 2010, when it was changed to be held only once a year in the spring semester since 2010. In 2006, one of my upper-intermediate Japanese students decided to join a Japanese speech contest. He worked very hard to prepare, and I assisted him individually. Despite my long history of teaching Japanese both in Australia and the United States, it was the first time one of my students participated in such a contest. My student competed at a level in which most of his competitors had studied abroad, but he had not. Though he did not win, it was very motivating for him, and it was a tremendous experience for both of us. Based on this experience, I discussed the idea of having our own speech contest at UNC Charlotte with the other staff members in the Japanese program.

Giving a speech in Japanese in front of a large audience is a big challenge for US students. However, being a contestant can be especially motivating for competitive students, and making a speech in a target language is incredibly helpful for developing oral skills. Thus, the Japanese program worked to recruit as many students as possible for the first speech contest. To encourage student participation, we reduced the burden by focusing less on speech quality and more on increasing participants. We thus set the standards of the contest quite low so as to not give too much extra burden to contestants. In the first few years all Japanese language learners at UNC Charlotte were eligible to compete, but as the years went on, too many students wanted to participate, so it became impossible to finish the contest within a reasonable amount of time. From that point forward, we limited contestants to those who had already completed at least one semester of Japanese. The length of speeches is kept very short and varies depending on level, for example, elementary level students speak for two minutes or less, and higher levels speak for three minutes. Furthermore, students do not have to write new scripts for the contest. Rather, they are allowed to use journals or essays that they have previously written for one of their Japanese classes. However, contestants are required to memorize their scripts as part of the nature of the speech contest.

Students are not forced to participate in or attend the speech contest, but they are encouraged to do so. For example, contestants are given one extra bonus point in their Japanese classes. We ask all learners, even noncontestants, to participate and support their classmates by coming and listening to the speeches, and allow students to make up one absence by doing so. In order to ascertain who came to listen to the speeches, and to give audience members something active to do for their own education, audience members receive a "make-up attendance sheet," and are required to write their names, their instructor's name and the rough content of five speakers' speeches either in English or in Japanese. Only participants who submit the sheet with all of the appropriate information can receive makeup credit. Students who are contestants and submit the sheet can receive two bonus points.

The hardest part of this event is to recruit contestants from every class. Simply announcing the speech contest in class generally results in no contestants. Instructors must therefore try to persuade students to compete over the course of several weeks. Because students are allowed to use old journal entries or essays that they have already written in class for their speech, interested students are asked to select one that might be suitable, and submit it to their instructor. Instructors revise student papers to be a suitable length and improve them to make them more appropriate as speeches as necessary. This process takes approximately one month, and students receive feedback on their scripts from their instructors about ten days prior to the speech contest. Students are then instructed on how to read their scripts properly, and asked to memorize them. Although students are allowed to bring the script with them on stage, in essence, they are not supposed to read the script, as they are judged partially on how well the memorized their script.

The program requests Japanese native speakers who are not familiar with the language learners to judge the contest. They are asked to rate four criteria from one to five: pronunciation, fluency, memorization and impression. The total scores of the three judges decide the top three contestants for each level. Winners receive a certificate of commendation and a $10 gift card, while second and third place winners receive a certificate and a $5 gift card. The money for the gift cards is subsidized by the Office of International Programs.

In 2019 I invited Japanese study abroad students as contestants at our speech contest for the first time, provided that they make a speech in English. When I announced this event to Japanese students, nobody was interested in it at first and all of them thought it to be too overwhelming because they would have to give their speech in their L2 to an audience of native speakers. Although I could understand their nervousness, I repeatedly recommended this opportunity to make a positive memory in their study abroad experiences. Finally, four Japanese students accepted my invitation to be contestants in our speech contest. All of them tried their best to memorize their scripts. On the day of the speech contest, when Japanese contestants proceeded to the center of the stage, the whole audience was tremendously encouraging, giving great applause to each contestant and shouting out their names. I did not expect such enthusiastic support from the audience, and I suspect they did not either. Afterwards, all of the Japanese contestants reported to me that they were satisfied with performance and that it definitely became one of their best memories during their study abroad experiences. Only recently did we begin involving Japanese students as participants in our events, but it was found to have a tremendous effect on the alleviation of the poverty of opportunity problem for our US students who are excited to see Japanese students also trying their best. Since then, as many Japanese students as possible have been invited to our events, such as the speech contest, year-end presentations, and student organizations, for example, the Nihon Club. The UNC Charlotte Japanese Speech Contest has become one of the biggest events in the Japanese program there.

In 2017 we received information on a Japanese speech contest called "J.Live Talk," sponsored by George Washington University. "J.Live Talk" is a new style of the speech contest in which contestants use PowerPoint to give their presentations. When introducing this contest to over intermediate-level learners, one student applied and sent a video application with which instructors were not allowed to help students. Despite the fact that he applied to the intermediate level, he was selected as one of the three advanced-level candidates. He tried his best to improve his pronunciation and speaking skills with great support from the entire Japanese program. A rehearsal was arranged for him a few days prior to the contest with myself and other Japanese instructors. As the first prize for each level was a round-trip air ticket to Japan, he was very excited about the possibility of winning and did his best to memorize the script perfectly. Although he did not win first place, he did get second, which is still very impressive. He also showed off his great accomplishment to his peers at that year's year-end presentations event, giving his speech again there. Later, feedback from other instructors indicated that their students were extremely inspired by his presentation. In this way, when lower-level learners observe advanced-level learners' speeches, they become motivated and want to give speeches and performances like the upperclassman, who they admire. Instructors were pleased to know that their students were highly motivated even if they only attended and listened to the speech contest. In reflection, I believe that implementing a speech contest at UNC Charlotte has been immensely beneficial for the Japanese program.

# Conclusion and recommendations

One of my favorite Japanese sayings is "*Suki koso mono no joozu nare*" (What you like you will do well). This quote suggests that motivation is the driving force in any situation and is the basis of my personal teaching philosophy. If given a job to do, most people don't mind spending numerous hours working at it if they love doing it. However, even if a task is not particularly difficult, people tend to procrastinate, give minimal effort, and otherwise not work diligently if they dislike it. Thus, in my own Japanese teaching, I feel that I must place a priority on getting my students to adore and love studying Japanese. Therein lies the true path to longevity in learning, and thus I have concentrated my talents and techniques toward doing so. This is in fact, the premise on which I have invested so much time into integrating the strategies and activities into the courses in the Japanese program that are presented throughout this book. Although the ultimate goal of many students (mastering Japanese or acquiring a high level of proficiency) may seem overwhelming to them at first, I want all of them to feel a sense of accomplishment in achieving smaller goals in hopes that they will then proceed to the next higher step.

The strategies introduced in Chapters 1 to 5 are major undertakings that I have enacted in accordance with my teaching philosophy, the most prominent issue of which is to increase learner's motivation levels. In the case of minor FLs, the most important hurdle to overcome here is the poverty of opportunity. Being able to utilize the skills that they learned in class is a true pleasure for students and also for instructors as well, so creating opportunities to do so provides them with experiences that enhance the motivation levels of students and drives their desire to go further, which in turn helps with the poverty of interest problem. Following this belief, it is my prerogative to provide my US learners of Japanese with occasions to speak in Japanese with native speakers. As outlined in this book, I have implemented several approaches to create such opportunities for them to converse and communicate with Japanese natives so that they feel satisfied with the gains they have made in learning. For example, Chapter 1 outlines how I created two teaching and learning methods that utilize Internet devices to provide learners with opportunities to contact native speakers, which ultimately also lead to improvements in participants' oral abilities. Furthermore, I have increased opportunity through inter-collaborative peer learning, as presented in Chapter 2, through collaborative project courses and a self-assessment and feedback project. I also worked to increase the number of chances to communicate with native speakers, as introduced in Chapter 3, through an LA program and a peer tutoring initiative. I have worked to increase both incoming Japanese students through a collaborative short-term visiting program at my university and bolstering the number of outgoing US students who study abroad in Japan, as discussed in Chapter 4. Finally, Chapter 5 presents two representative motivation-boosting extracurricular activities that I have created and integrated into the Japanese program. My experiences, the data presented in the chapters, and the theoretical background support the idea that these strategies are all effective in helping to enhance student motivation and overcome the problems of poverty of interest and poverty of opportunity that minor FL learners, such as US learners of Japanese at UNC Charlotte, face. However, the best indication of the effectiveness of the efforts and programs I have reported on in this book is the rate at which the Japanese program at UNC Charlotte has grown, against all odds.

One of the most difficult FLs for English native speaker is the Japanese language. While there is some interest in Japan and Japanese culture in the United States, the rates of enrollment have been decreasing, especially in areas where Japanese is a minor FL, such as the southeastern area of the United States. However, despite these difficulties, the Japanese program at UNC Charlotte has not suffered a decrease in registered students as many Japanese programs in the United States have over the past two decades. Instead, the number of enrollees has been increasing, more courses have been added, and where the language was only offered as a minor in the past, now students can major in it and receive a Japanese BA degree, and moreover a Japanese BA Honors degree. I feel that much of this has been due to the efforts that my colleagues and I have taken to battle the poverty of opportunity and poverty of interest that many of our students struggle with through a number of innovative strategies.

Students of minor FLs often face similar difficulties, and I think that helping and motivating students starts with the teacher. At UNC Charlotte, once students begin studying Japanese, I want each and every one of them to achieve their goals. Some students want to graduate with a Japanese BA degree, whereas others may only want a minor, or simply to become moderately proficient in the language. Some students' dream of studying abroad in Japan, and others simply want to study Japanese anime or culture, or fulfill a FL requirement as a part of their general education requirements. Whatever their goal is, once they register for the Japanese program, I do not want them to give up in the middle by withdrawing or receiving a failing grade. In order to prevent this, I have designed a curriculum, several strategies, and extracurricular activities that have been integrated into

*Conclusion and recommendations* 103

the Japanese program over the last two decades that will motivate students so that they continue studying. This book has focused on the practical aspects of integration, detailing the procedures so that teachers of other minor FLs can mimic them, and shown their effective outcomes. It also offers ideas on how to inspire learners to continue studying by providing supporting programs that encourage learners to accomplish their goals. Although the book often touches on these issues by using my own record as a teacher of Japanese in the southeastern area of the United States as a practical case study, these various countermeasures have worked together to heighten our learners' motivation at my institution, and can surely be adapted for other minor FL teachers.

For instructors or other faculty members looking to support a minor FL program, I recommend thinking about student motivation first and foremost when selecting which strategies to implement. I feel motivation, specifically intrinsic motivation, is of the utmost importance because if motivation levels are increased high enough, students will progress with their studies autonomously, without needing any special attention from instructors. No matter how much natural talent students may have at learning FLs, if they do not spend enough time with the language, they surely cannot master it. Students who have successfully achieved their goals surely made great efforts when no one was looking, and motivation was the force behind this sort of drive. Furthermore, motivation is also what will help teachers to lower attrition rates, attract more students, and grow their programs, much in the way that the Japanese program at UNC Charlotte has.

Finally, I advise instructors looking to grow minor FL programs to think about motivating not only students but also their fellow faculty members as well. One of my firm beliefs to managing an educational department is to strengthen mutual understanding amongst all of the staff working within it. Therefore, I try to do my best to build and maintain a friendly group relationship amongst our staff members. I do this because program growth is impossible if the teachers who are running it do not have consensus on the goals and aims of our program. It is essential that everyone involved be solidly united toward the same objective. I have seen the progress of similar groups and organizations come to a grinding halt because there is no unity, which makes them unable to face problems when they arise and eventually leads to them breaking down. Thus, in the Japanese program at UNC Charlotte, we have staff meetings once a week to talk about student problems, class management, extra-curricular activities planning, and to reflect after events in order to improve upon them further. I generally provide little snacks, for example, candies, cookies, or drinks, to make sure the atmosphere remains a friendly one. We are able to come up with excellent solutions because we all discuss problems together, rather than trying to solve them individually. As the proverb says, "Out of the counsel of three comes wisdom."

In order to further improve staff relations, a few days prior to the beginning of the semester, we all have lunch together and talk about our holidays and things that we cannot normally discuss with our busy schedules during the semester. Whenever we have good news, we disseminate it to everyone and are genuinely happy for one another. When we have newcomers, we spend time supporting them so that they can adapt themselves to the new environment easily. After finishing the semester, we share another meal together in order to reward ourselves for our efforts during the semester. Furthermore, once every few years I invite all of the staff and their families to have dinner at my home. Such a relaxed and amicable atmosphere helps us to become familiar with one another, which contributes to a closer relationship amongst the staff. Sharing meals and conversations with each other is the key to internal harmony. It is imperative to build these relationships to encourage communication amongst staff. The warm environment also permeates to the students in the program, which is required for their motivation. I believe that this kind of harmony results in solutions whenever staff or students have problems, whether it is in the classroom or their daily lives. Therefore, I constantly do my best to create a teaching and learning environment where everyone can work enjoyably in peace of mind.

# Postscript

The first thing that comes to mind regarding the publishing of this book is how the numerous strategies have been integrated one after another into the Japanese program for the last 17 years at UNC Charlotte. All of these endeavors were meant to provide students with enjoyable moments and satisfying experiences and to improve their motivation levels. My desire has been that all of our students continue to study Japanese and proceed to the next higher level of classes. Whenever I try to incorporate a new strategy into our course or program, it is essential to know how it affected our students, whether it was accepted by our students, and whether it was effective or efficient for students through assisting their learning, solving their problems, responding to their questions, or inspiring students for further studies. Therefore, I conduct a research study to determine whether the new strategy has turned out beneficial or helpful for our students. Such studies are very important, as it may not be possible for us to find if students were pleased or disfavor it, and we must always strive to do what is best for the students. Strategies that are not accepted by students are discontinued immediately. On the other hand, if the strategy is clearly shown to be effective and was accepted by students as a helpful device, we continue it in the program, even though it may be time-consuming for instructors and require a lot of effort on their part.

One example of an intervention is a UNC Charlotte Japanese speech contest. Only the Japanese program among many foreign language programs in my department has been holding a speech contest every year continuously for many years because the event obviously provides our students with abundant benefits. I sometimes hear from other professors, "We used to have a speech contest in my own program in the past, but I stopped it because it required a great deal of effort which interfered with our time for research." Certainly, university professors are reluctant to engage in activities which occupy their time. While I have struggled with such policies and my own teaching policies, I have tried my best to continue such programs that influences positively for students.

Although there were only two faculty members working in the Japanese program at UNC Charlotte 17 years ago, I now tremendously enjoy working together with nine other teaching professors who are like a big family to me. Remembering these 17 years at UNC Charlotte, I have really had a variety of memories during this time, and although there were also a lot of bitter memories, sadness, disappointment, struggling and suffering because I could not overcome difficulties that I faced, the pleasures, great excitements, big surprises, compliments and great honors from the department, university through awarding three kinds of recognition, American Association of Teachers of Japanese and also Japanese government for overshadow them. If I had to do it all by myself, it would be definitely impossible to conduct and accomplish so much, but through tight cooperation amongst our staff, we have been able to implement plentiful strategies and activities into our program to achieve our final goal: fostering our students' drive to ultimately enhance and grow our program.

All of my Japanese colleagues have worked hard on my behalf, and I have received great cooperation toward my teaching policies. Without such distinct teamwork in our program, I could not have reached such a brilliant achievement, and so I am eternally grateful to all of my staff and colleagues here. Therefore, I wish to extend my thanks to all of my colleagues for their super cooperation and dedication along the way. Also, I am thankful to the cooperation of all of the students learning in the Japanese program, whose cooperation and patience was quintessential to the success of the research studies described in this book. I would also like to extend my gratitude to the Chair of the Department of Languages and Culture Studies, Dr. Ann Gonzalez, who recognized the benefits of this project from the conceptual stage of this book. It is truly thanks to her continual support that my book was successfully published, and thus I would like to acknowledge her for her contributions to it. Without support from her, I absolutely could not have proceeded with or finished my book project. My sincere appreciation also goes to Dr. Ryan Spring, associate professor at Tohoku University, Japan, who has been implementing innovative educational methods together with me as a co-researcher for five years, provided tremendous assistance and extremely worthwhile advice regarding the publishing of this book. Fortunately for me, he accepted the job of editor of this book and was heavily involved through contributing backup and support in its publishing. It is with deep heartfelt acknowledgment and gratefulness that I wish to express my appreciation to him. My great appreciation also goes to the Japan Foundation from where I was awarded a grant to aid the project of getting this book published, specifically to Ms. Nakai who clearly understood the significance of it and tremendously supported me through providing appropriate instructions and excellent suggestions. It would be hard to have achieved my goal without her warm, kind and outstanding assistance. Lastly, I would like to express my sincere gratitude to my husband, Hidetoshi Kato, for walking along the path of writing my book and seeing me to the summit of my goal.

# References

Achmad, D., & Yusuf, Y.Q. (2014). Observing pair-work task in an English speaking class. *International Journal Instruction, 7*(1), 151–165.

Aguila, K.B., & Harajanto, I. (2016). Foreign language anxiety and its impacts on students' speaking competency. *Anima Indonesian Psychological Journal, 32*(1), 29–40.

Aida, Y. (1994). Examination of Horwitz, Horwitz, and Cope's construct of foreign language anxiety: The case of students of Japanese. *Modern Language Journal, 78*(2), 155–168.

Al-Mahrooqi, R.I., & Tabakow, M.L. (2015). Effectiveness of debate in ESL/EFL-content courses in the Arabian Gulf: A comparison of two recent student-centered studies in Oman and in Dubai, U.A.E. *21st Century Academic Forum Conference Proceeding 2015 Conference at Harvard, 5*(1), 417–428.

Amrein, A., & Peña, R.A. (2000). Asymmetry in dual language practice: Assessing imbalance in a program promoting equality. *Education Policy Analysis Archives, 8*(8), 1–17.

Bailey, J.M., & Vooheris-Sargent, A. (2018). Regional peer coaching program for basic science faculty. *Medical Science Educator, 28*, 773–776.

Beckett, G.H., & Miller, P.C. (2006). *Project-based second and foreign language education: Past, present and future*. Greenwich, CT: Information Age Publishing.

Beckett, G.H., & Slater, T. (2005). The Project framework: A tool for language, content and skills integration. *ELT Journal, 59*(2), 108–116.

Bell, S. (2010). Project-based learning for the 21st century: Skills for the future. *The Clearing House: A Journal of Educational Strategies, Issues and Ideas, 83*(2), 39–43.

Blake, R. (2008). *Brave new digital classroom: Technology and foreign language learning*. Washington, DC: Georgetown University Press.

Blue, G.M. (1994). Self-assessment of foreign language skills: Does it work? *CLE Working Papers, 3*, 18–35.

Blumenfeld, P.C., Soloway, E., Marx, R.W., Krajcik, J.S., Guzdial, M., & Palinscar, A. (1991). Motivating project-based learning: Sustaining the doing, supporting the learning. Educational Psychologist, 26(3–4), 369–398.

Canale, M., & Swain, M. (1980). Theoretical bases of communicative approaches to second language teaching and testing. *Applied Linguistics, 1*, 1–47.

Chaves, J.F., Baker, C.M., Chaves, J.A., & Fisher, M.L. (2006). Self, peer, and tutor assessments of MSN competencies using the PBL-evaluator. *Journal of Nursing Education, 45*(1), 25–31.

Christensen, J.D., Schmalz, N.A., Challyandra, L., & Stark, M.E. (2018). Establishment of a peer teaching assistant program for preclinical human gross anatomy curricula. *Medical Science Educator, 28,* 765–772.

The Chronicle List. (2019). Which colleges grant the most Bachelor's degrees in foreign languages? *The Chronicle of Higher Education.* January 29. Retrieved on May 29, 2019, from www.chronicle.com/article/Which-Colleges-Grant-the-Most/245567/?key=lUtmf4EyiX3iIy8Gt541ogWMHa1QaeW7kZesEMjRkb9zL60Vx1pP2NesIvCvIp3jSjViczdnSV9HbXlSZDd4MWt0NUoxLVFEQ3U1bkN6Rzl2Wms2Sk96YmprVQ#.XGLGT05UK0k.email.

Contreras Jr., E. (2015). Rhetoric and reality in study abroad: The aims of overseas study for U.S. higher education in the twentieth century. EdD dissertation, Harvard University.

Csizér, K., & Dörnyei, Z. (2005). The internal structure of language learning motivation and its relationship with language choice and learning effort. *Modern Language Journal, 89*(1), 19–36.

D'Andrea, V.-M. (1996). Starting a teaching assistants' training programme: Lessons learned in the USA. *Journal of Geography in Higher Education, 20*(1), 89–100.

Daniel, S.J., Xie, F., & Kedia, B.L. (2014). 2014 U.S. business needs for employees with international expertise. NAFSA Executive Summary. Retrieved on September 14, 2019, from www.nafsa.org/policy-and-advocacy/policy-resources/trends-us-study-abroad.

Dauer, R.M. (1983). Stress-timing and syllable-timing reanalyzed. *Journal of Phonetics, 11,* 51–62.

DiMaggio, L.M. (2016). An analysis of study abroad as a factor to increase student engagement and reduce dropouts in higher education institutions. Dissertation for EdD, Saint Peter's University.

Dooly, M., & Sadler, R. (2016). Becoming little scientists: Technologically-enhanced project-based language learning. *Language Learning & Technology, 20*(1), 54–78.

Dörnyei, Z. (2001a). New themes and approaches in second language motivation research. *Annual Review of Applied Linguistics, 21,* 43–59.

Dörnyei, Z. (2001b). *Teaching and researching motivation.* Harlow, UK: Longman.

Dvorak, A.M.W., Christiansen, L.D., Fischer, N.L., & Underhill, J.B. (2011). A necessary partnership: Study abroad and sustainability in higher education. *Frontiers: The Interdisciplinary Journal of Study Abroad, 21,* 143–166.

Ehrman, M.E. (1996). *Understanding second language learning difficulties.* London: Sage.

Ellis, R. (1985). *Understanding second language acquisition.* New York: Oxford University Press.

Entzinger, J.O., Morimura, K., & Suzuki, S. (2013). Virtual and real exchange with overseas universities to enhance language and learning. *JSEE Annual Conference International Session Proceedings,* 16–21. Retrieved on March 30, 2016, from https://ci.nii.ac.jp/naid/110009674699/en.

Farouck, I. (2016). A project-based language learning model for improving the Willingness to communicate of EFL students. *Systemics, Cybernetics and Informatics, 14*(2), 11–18.

Forester, L.A., & Meyer, E. (2015). Implementing student-produced video projects in language courses. *Underrichtspraxis, 48*(2), 192–210.

Freeman, R. (2000). Contextual challenges to dual-language education: A case study of a developing middle school program. *Anthropology & Education Quarterly, 31*(2), 202–229.

Gabb, S. (2001). Authentic goal settings with ABE learners: Accountability for programs or process for learning. *Adventures in Assessment, 13*, 17–23.

Gardner, R.C. (1985). *Social psychology and second language learning: The role of attitudes and motivation.* London, ON: Edward Arnold.

Gardner, R.C. (2001). Language learning motivation: The student, the teacher, and the researcher. *Texas Papers in Foreign Language Education, 6*(1), 1–18.

Gardner, R.C., & Lambert, W. (1972). *Attitudes and motivation in second language learning.* Rowley, MA: Newbury House.

Gerena, L., & Keiler, L. (2012). Effective intervention with urban secondary English language learners: How peer instructors support learning. *Bilingual Research Journal, 35*(1), 76–97.

Gergen, K.J. (1999). *An invitation to social construction.* Thousand Oaks, CA: Sage.

Godwin-Jones, R. (2013). Integrating intercultural competence into language learning through technology. *Language Learning & Technology, 17*(2), 1–11.

Gutiérrez, K.D., Baquedano-Lopez, P., Alvarez, H.H., & Chiu, M.M. (1999). Building a culture of collaboration through hybrid language practices. *Theory into Practice, 38*(2), 87–93.

Güller, M.G., Keskin, M.E., Döyen, A., & Akyer, H. (2015). On teaching assistant-task assignment problem: A case study. *Computers & Industrial Engineering, 79*, 18–26.

Hafner, C.A., Li, D.C.S., & Miller, L. (2015). Language choice among peers in project-based learning: A Hong Kong case study of English language learners' plurilingual practices in out-of-class computer-mediated communication. *Canadian Modern Language Review, 71*(4), 441–470.

Harris, M. (1997). Self-assessment of language learning in formal settings. *ELT Journal, 51*(1), 12–20.

Hernández, T.A. (2010). Promoting speaking proficiency through motivation and interaction: The study abroad and classroom learning contexts. *Foreign Language Annals, 43*, 650–670.

Hilsdon, J. (2014). Peer learning for change in higher education. *Innovation in Education and Teaching International, 51*(3), 244–254.

Hinds, J. (1987). Reader versus writer responsibility: A new typology. In U. Connor and R. Kaplan (eds.), *Writing across cultures: Analysis of L2 text* (pp. 141–152). Reading, MA: Addison-Wesley.

Howard, E.R., Sugarman, J., & Christian, D. (2003). *Trends in two-way immersion education: A review of the research.* Washington, DC: Institute of Education Sciences.

Hyland, F. (2001). Providing effective support: Investigating feedback to distance language learners. *Open Learning, 16*(3), 233–247.

The Japan Agency for Cultural Affairs. (2010). *Kaitei Joyo Kanji-hyo* [The Revised List of Kanji in Regular Usage]. Retrieved on August 30, 2019, from www.bunka.go.jp/seisaku/bunkashingikai/sokai/sokai_10/pdf/kaitei_kanji_toushin.pdf.

The Japan Foundation. (2017). *Survey report on Japanese-language education abroad 2015.* Tokyo: Independent Administrative Agency, The Japan Foundation.

Johnson, S. (2019). Colleges lose a "stunning" 651 foreign-language programs in 3 years. The Chronicle of Higher Education, January 22, 2019. Retrieved on July 23, 2019, from www.chronicle.com/article/Colleges-Lose-a-Stunning-/245526.

Jon, J.-E., Shin, Y.-J., & Fry, G.W. (2018). Understanding study abroad participants' career decisions and perspectives in US higher education. *Compare: A Journal of Comparative and International Education*, September 17, 2018, 1–18. Retrieved on September 14, 2019, from https://doi.org/10.1080/03057925.2018.1502608.

Jordan, E.H., & Lambert, R.D. (1991). *Japanese language instruction in the USA: Resources, practice, and investment strategy*. Washington, DC: The National Foreign Language Center.

Kato, F. (2000). *Introducing learning strategies, time management, and anxiety-free learning in basic Japanese: An intervention study*. PhD dissertation, University of Sydney.

Kato, F. (2002). Efficacy of intervention strategies in learning success rates. *Foreign Language Annals*, 35(1), 61–72.

Kato, F. (2007). A comparative study of motivation: Foreign language learners of Spanish, French, German and Japanese in tertiary education. *Studies in Language Sciences*, 6, 97–112.

Kato, F. (2009). Student preferences: Goal-setting and self-assessment activities in a tertiary education environment. *Language Teaching Research*, 13(2), 177–200.

Kato, F. (2010). *Improving student motivation toward Japanese learning*. Tokyo: Gakujutsu Shuppankai.

Kato, F. (2016). Enhancing integrative motivation: The Japanese-American collaborative learning project. *Cogent Education*, 3(1), 1–15.

Kato, F. (2018a). Integrating a debate activity into an intermediate Japanese class: A practice report through learner's report. *Postscript*, 34(1), 1–22.

Kato, F. (2018b). Innovations in integrating language assistants: Inter-collaborative learning. *Journal of Language Education*, 4(4), 54–62.

Kato, F., Spring, R., & Mori, C. (2016). Mutually beneficial foreign language learning: Creating meaningful interactions through video-synchronous computer-mediated communication. *Foreign Language Annals*, 49(2), 355–366.

Kato, F., Spring, R., & Mori, C. (forthcoming). Incorporating project-based language learning into distance learning: Creating a home page during computer-mediated learning sessions. *Language Teaching Research*.

Kibler, A., Salerno, A., & Hardigree, C. (2014). "More than being in a class": Adolescents' ethnolinguistic insights in a two-way dual language program. *Language and Education*, 28(3), 251–275.

Korinek, K., Howard, J.A., & Bridges, G.S. (1999). "Train the whole scholar": A developmental based program for teaching assistant training in sociology. *Teaching Sociology*, 27, 343–359.

Kost, C. (2008). Innovations in teaching assistant development: An apprenticeship model. *Foreign Language Annals*, 41(1), 29–68.

Ladefoged, P. (1975). *A course in phonetics*. New York: Harcourt Brace Jovanovich.

Laurillard, D. (1993). *Rethinking university teaching a framework for the effective use of educational technology*. London: Routledge.

Lee, R.E. (1998). Assessing retention program holding power effectiveness across smaller community colleges. *Journal of College Student Development*, 29(3), 255–262.

Liskin-Gasparro, J.E. (1982). *ETS oral proficiency testing manual*. Princeton, NJ: Educational Testing Service.

Liu, X. (2016). Motivation management of project-based learning for business English adult learners. *International Journal of Higher Education*, 5(3), 137–145.

Lockspeiser, T.M., O'Sullivan, P., Teherani, A., & Muller, J. (2008). Understanding the experience of being taught by peers: The value of social and cognitive congruence. *Advances in Health Science Education, 13,* 361–372.

Lynch, T., & Maclean, J. (2003). Effects of feedback on performance: A study of advanced learners on an ESP speaking course. *Edinburgh Working Papers in Applied Linguistics, 12,* 19–44.

MacIntyre, P.D., & Gardner, R.C. (1994). The subtle effects of language anxiety on cognitive processing in the second language. *Language Learning, 44,* 283–305.

MacIntyre, P.D., Noels K.A., & Clément, R. (1997). Biases in self-ratings of second language proficiency: The role of language anxiety. *Language Learning, 47*(2), 265–287.

Maftoon, P., Birjandi, P., & Ahmadi, A. (2013). The relationship between project-based instruction and motivation: A study of EFL learners in Iran. *Theory and Practice in Language Studies, 3*(9), 1630–1638.

Masgoret, A.M., & Gardner, R.C. (2003). Attitudes, motivation, and second language learning: A meta-analysis of studies conducted by Gardner and associates. *Language Learning, 53,* 123–163.

Mewis, K., Dee, J., Lam, V., Obdradovich, S., & Cassidy, A. (2018). A new self-assessment teaching assistant survey for growth and development. *Teaching and Learning Inquiry, 6*(1), 79–90.

Miles, M.B., & Huberman, A.M. (1994). Qualitative data analysis. London: Sage.

Moritz, C.E.B. (1996). *Student self-assessment of language proficiency: Perceptions of self and others.* Paper presented at the Annual Meeting of the American Association for Applied Linguistics, Chicago, IL.

Moust, J.H.C., & Schmidt, H.G. (1994). Facilitating small-group learning: A comparison of student and staff tutors' behavior. *Instructional Science, 22,* 287–301.

Murray, R.W. (1996). The teaching assistant. *Analytical Chemistry of News & Features, 68*(23), 709A.

NAFSA. (2014). Trends in U.S. Study Abroad. Retrieved on September 14, 2019, from www.nafsa.org/policy-and-advocacy/policy-resources/trends-us-study-abroad.

Niser, J.C. (2010). Study abroad education in New England higher education: A pilot study. *International Journal of Educational Management, 24*(1), 48–55.

Norris-Holt, J. (2001). Motivation as a contributing factor in second language acquisition. *The Internet TESL Journal.* Retrieved on August 20, 2019, from http://iteslj.org/Articles/Norris-Motivation.html.

Oxford, R.L. (1996). *Language learning motivation: Pathways to the new century.* Honolulu: University of Hawai'i Press, Second Language Teaching and Curriculum Center.

Oxford, R.L. (1999). Anxiety and the language learner: New insights. In J. Arnold (ed.), *Affect in language learning* (pp. 58–67). London: Cambridge University Press.

Oxford, R.L., Park-Oh, Y., Ito, S., & Sumrall, M. (1993). Japanese by satellite: Effects of motivation, language learning styles and strategies, gender, course level, and previous language learning experience on Japanese language achievement. *Foreign Language Annals, 26*(3), 359–371.

Oxford, R.L., & Shearin, J. (1996). Language learning motivation in a new key. In R.L. Oxford (ed.), *Language learning motivation: Pathways to new century* (pp. 121–144). Honolulu: University of Hawai'i, Second Language Teaching and Curriculum Center.

Ozek, Y. (2009). Overseas teaching experience: Student teachers' perspectives of teaching practicum. *Procedia Social and Behavioral Sciences, 1*, 2541–2545.

Paige, R.M., Fry, G.W., Stallman, E.M., Josic, J., & Jon, J.-E. (2009). Study abroad for global engagement: Long-term impact of mobility experiences. *Intercultural Education, 20*(1), 529–544.

Pardjono, P. (2002). Active learning: The Dewey, Piaget, Vygotsky, and constructivist theory perspectives. *Jurnal Ilmu Pendidikan, 9*(3), 163–178.

Pintrich, P.R., Smith, D.A.F., Garcia, T., & Mckeachie, W. (1993). Reliability and predictive validity of the motivated strategies for learning questionnaire (MSLQ). *Educational and Psychological Measurement, 53*, 801–813.

Qureshi, M.A., & Stormyhr, E. (2012). Group dynamics and peer-tutoring a pedagogical tool for learning in higher education. *International Education Studies, 5*(2), 118–124.

Ratminingsih, N.M. (2015). The use of personal photographs in writing in project-based language learning: A case study. *The New English Teacher, 9*(1), 102–118.

Rubin, J. (2003). Diary writing as a process: Simple, useful, powerful. *Guidelines, 25*(2), 10–14.

Rubin, J., & Thompson, I. (1994). *How to be a more successful language learner.* Boston: Heinle & Heinle.

Ryder, G., Russell, P., Burton, M., Quinn, P., & Daly, S. (2017). Embedding peer support as a core learning skill in higher education. *Journal of Information Literacy, 11*(1), 184–203.

Sahin, M. (2008). Cross-cultural experience in preservice teacher education. *Teaching and Teacher Education, 24*, 1777–1790.

Saito, Y., & Samimy, K.K. (1996). Foreign language anxiety and language performance: A study of learner anxiety in beginning, intermediate, and advanced-level college students of Japanese. *Foreign Language Annals, 29*(2), 239–251.

Sakai, Y. (1995). Self evaluation of mathematics course students and the evaluation by their instructors in practice teaching. Teaching practicum education guidance center. Research Bulletin, 19, 1–11.

Samimy, K.K., & Tabuse, M. (1992). Affective variables and a less commonly taught language: A study in beginning Japanese classes. *Language Learning, 42*(3), 377–398.

Scarcella, R.C., & Oxford, R.L. (1992). *The tapestry of language learning: The individual in the communicative classroom.* Boston: Heinle & Heinle.

Schunk, D.H., & Swartz, C.W. (1993). Goals and progress feedback: Effects on self-efficacy and writing achievement. *Contemporary Educational Psychology, 18*, 337–354.

Shi, X. (2011). Negotiating power and access to second language resources: A study of short-term Chinese MBA students in America. *Modern Language Journal, 95*(4), 575–588.

Spring, R., & Horie, K. (2013). How cognitive typology affects second language acquisition: A study of Japanese and Chinese learners of English. *Cognitive Linguistics, 24*(4), 689–710.

Spring, R., Kato, F., & Mori, C. (2019). Factors associated with improvement in oral fluency when using video-synchronous mediated communication with native speakers: An analysis of 3 years of data from a Skype-partner program. *Foreign Language Annals, 52*(1), 87–100.

Stone, P. (2012). Implications of a socio-cultural context for the co-construction of talk in a task-based English as a foreign language classroom in Japan. *Classroom Discourse, 3*(1), 65–82.

Storch, N., & Aldosali, A. (2012). Learners' use of first language (Arabic) in pair work in an EFL class. *Language Teaching Research, 14*(4), 355–375.

Taillefer, L., & Munoz-Luna, R. (2014). Developing oral skills through Skype: A language project analysis. *Procedia – Social and Behavioral Science, 141,* 260–264.

Tajes, M., & Ortiz, J. (2010). Assessing study abroad programs: Application of the "SLEPT" framework through learning communities. *Journal of General Education, 59*(1), 17–41.

Tian, J., & Wang, Y. (2010). Taking language learning outside the classroom: Learners' perspectives of eTandem learning via Skype. *Innovation in Language Learning and Teaching, 4,* 181–197.

Todd, R.W. (2002). Using self-assessment for evaluation. *English Teaching Forum, 40*(1), 16–19.

Tohsaku, Y. (2007, March). *How to improve your teaching through assessment.* Paper presented at the meeting of the South East Association of Teachers of Japanese, Memphis, TN.

Topping, K. (1996). The effectiveness of peer tutoring in further and higher education: A typology and review of the literature. *Higher Education, 32,* 321–345.

Towndrow, P., & Vallance, M. (2004). *Using IT in the language classroom.* Singapore: Longman.

Trembly, P.F., & Gardner, R.C. (1995). Expanding the motivation construct in language learning. *Modern Language Journal, 79*(4), 505–518.

Tsunoda, T. (2009). *Sekai no gengo to Nihongo: Gengo ruikeiron kara mita Nihongo* [The world's languages and Japanese: Japanese as seen from a linguistic typology]. Tokyo: Kuroshio.

Tung, R.L. (1998). American expatriates abroad: From neophytes to cosmopolitans. *Journal of World Business, 33*(2), 125–144.

Varner, I.I., & Palmer, T.M. (2002). Successful expatriation and organizational strategies. *Review of Business, Spring,* 8–11.

Vygotsky, L.S. (1978). *Mind and society: The development of higher mental processes.* Cambridge, MA: Harvard University Press.

Warschauer, M., & De Florio-Hansen, I. (2003). Multilingualism, identity and the Internet. In A. Hu and I. De Florio-Hansen (eds.), *Multiple identity and multilingualism* (pp. 155–179). Tübingen, Germany: Stauffenburg.

Wiese, A.-M. (2004). Bilingualism and biliteracy for all? Unpacking two-way immersion as second grade. *Language and Education, 18*(1), 69–92.

Willard-Holt, C. (2001). The impact of a short-term international field experience on preservice teachers. *Teaching and Teacher Education, 24*(1), 14–25.

Woo, Y., & Reeves, T.C. (2006). Meaningful interaction in web-based learning: A social constructivist interpretation. *The Internet and Higher Education, 10,* 15–25.

Yang, N. (2005). Higher education in global economy: A study abroad comparison. *Proceedings of the Academy of Educational Leadership, 10*(1), 77–78.

Yang, N.D. (1998). Exploring a new role for teachers: Promoting learner autonomy. *System, 26,* 127–135.

Yang, Y.C., Gamble, J., & Tang, S.S. (2012). Voice-over instant messaging as a tool for enhancing the oral proficiency and motivation of English-as-a-foreign-language learners. *British Journal of Educational Technology, 43*, 448–464.

Youngs, B.L., & Green, A. (2001). A successful peer writing assistant program. *Foreign Language Annals, 34*(6), 550–558.

Zare, P., & Othman, M. (2013). Classroom debate as a systematic teaching/learning approach. *World Applied Sciences Journal, 28*(11), 1506–1513.

# Index

*Note*: Page numbers in *italics* indicate figures and in **bold** indicate tables on the corresponding pages.

Ahmadi, A. 22
American Council on the Teaching of Foreign Languages (ACTFL) 15, 35
Amrein, A. 32, 33
attrition rates, language assistant programs to reduce 44, 48, 53–63
autonomy, learner *11*, 21, 31, 44

Baker, C.M. 33
Birjandi, P. 22
Blumenfeld, P.C. 24, 29

Center for Research on the Education of Students Placed at Risk 32
Chaves, J.A. 33, 38
Chaves, J.F. 33, 38
China 6
Chinese 5–8, 15, 46
*Chronicle of Higher Education* 9
collaborative short-term visiting programs 74–77, 80, 82–84, 102

Dooly, M. 12, 21, 22
Dörnyei, Z. 3, 4, 74, 75
double immersion teaching approach 32, 33

educational strategies: inter-collaborative peer learning 11, 31–49, **36**, 88; interventions to enhance learner autonomy and motivation *11*; introduction to 31
Ellis, R. 12–14, 31
extracurricular activities: introduction to 93; Japanese speech contest 97–99, 105; semester-end presentations **95**, 95–97; year-end presentations 55, 67, 93, 97, 99, 100
extrinsic motivation 4

Farouck, I. 22
feedback 20, 31, 44–48
Fisher, M.L. 33
Freeman 32, 33
French 2, 5, 7

Gabb, S. 48
Gardner, R.C. 2–4, 6, 74, 75
German 2, 5, 7, 8
Green, A. 65, 67
Gutiérrez, K.D. 33, 34
Guzdial, M. 24

Hafner, C.A. 21, 22
Harris, M. 44, 46
Hilsdon, J. 58, 64, 65, 67, 68
Howard, E.R. 32, 33
Howard, J.A. 53
Huberman, A.M. 18, 28, 41, 56, 78
Hyland, F. 44, 45, 47

instrumental motivation 2, 6, 75, 78
integrative motivation 6, 74–79, 81, 82
inter-collaborative peer learning 10, *11*, 31, 32, 34, **36**, 39, 40, 42, 43, 49, 88; advice for offering 42, 43; conclusions from example study on 41, 42; course content 35–39, **36**, **38**; example of university level 34–39, **36**, **38**; indications of success with 39–41; theory behind 32–34
intrinsic motivation 4, 29, 31, 38, 65, 75, 103

Japanese: background of learning and circumstances at UNC Charlotte 6, 7; degree of difficulty of learning 9; problems for learners of, at UNC Charlotte 7–9; strategies to enhance student motivation for learning 3–5, 9–11, *11*, 101–104; at UNC Charlotte as case study 5, 7
Japanese speech contest 55, 93, 97–100, 105
Japan Foundation 6, 106
Jon, J.-E. 85, 86, 88, 90

Kato, F. 2, 4, 13, 14, 16–23, 27–29, 32, 36, 42, 47, 54, 56, 59–61, 74–76, 78–82, 106
Kibler, A. 32–34
Krajcik, J.S. 24

language assistants (LAs): advice for creating and implementing programs with 62, 63; conclusions from case study on 60–61; differing from traditional TAs 54–56; effects of 56–60; introduction to 53, 54
Laurillard, D. 44, 45
learner autonomy *see* autonomy, learner
learning management systems (LMS) 48
Liu, X. 22
Lynch, T. 44, 45, 47

Maclean, J. 44, 45, 47
Maftoon, P. 22
Marx, R.W. 24
Mewis, K. 53, 54
Miles, M.B. 18, 28, 41, 56, 78
minor foreign language: challenges for programs in 2, 3; defined 1, 2; increasing motivation for learning 3–5; Japanese as, in Charlotte 7, 8
Moritz, C.E.B. 44
motivation 3–5, 101–104; educational strategies for (*see* educational strategies); extracurricular activities and (*see* extracurricular activities); increased through collaborative short-term visiting programs *11*, 74–84, **83**; language assistants (*see* language assistants (LAs)); peer tutoring and (*see* peer tutor programs); strategies to enhance 9–11, *11*; study abroad programs and (*see* study abroad programs); technology strategies for (*see* technology strategies)
Moust, J.H.C. 58, 64

National Association of Foreign Student Affairs (NAFSA) 86
Niser, J.C. 86
Norris-Holt, J. 82

Ortiz, J. 85, 86, 88, 90
Oxford, R.L. 1–4, 12–14, 31, 74

Palinscar, A. 24
peer tutor programs: advice for integrating 68–69; case study of 65–67, **66**; conclusions from case study on 68; effects of 67, 68; introduction to 63, 64; literature on 64, 65; log 72
Peña, R.A. 33
poverty of interest problem: extracurricular activities for 93–100; peer tutor programs for 63–69; self-assessment and receiving feedback for 44–49
poverty of interest and poverty of opportunity problems: inter-collaborative peer learning for 31–43; project-based language learning for 21–30; short-term visiting programs for *11*, 74–85; study abroad programs 85–91
poverty of opportunity problem: language assistant programs for 53–63; VSCMC learning programs for 13–21
project-based language learning (PBLL): advice for creating VSCMC combined with 29, 30; case study of VSCMC-integrated 22–24, *25*, *26*; conclusions from case study on 28, 29; indications of success in 25–28; theoretical motivation for implementing 21, 22

Ratminingsih, N.M. 22
Reeves, T.C. 14

Sadler, R. 12, 21, 22
Saito, Y. 4
Samimy, K.K. 3, 4
Scarcella, R.C. 1, 2, 12–14, 31
Schmidt, H.G. 58, 64

Schunk, D.H. 44, 45
self-assessment and feedback: advice for introducing interventions in 48, 49; conclusions from example study on 48; theory behind 44, 45; UNC Charlotte project in 45–48
short-term visiting programs *see* motivation
Skype partner programs *11*, 13–17, 19–22, 31, 32; advice for creating 19–21; conclusions on 19; indications of success with 16–19; project-based language learning and 13, 21
Soloway, E. 24
Spanish 1, 5, 6, 8, 9, 32, 33
speech contest 55, 93, 97–100
Spring, R. 8, 13, 20, 28, 32, 39, 40, 106
study abroad programs: advice for creating and conducting 83–85; case study on 75, 76; discussions and conclusions from data on 82, 83, **83**; importance of institutional partnerships and 85–91; increasing integrative motivation through 74–85, **83**; introduction to 74; preliminary project 76, 77; preliminary project outcomes 77–80; revised project 80; two year comparison of 80–82
Swartz, C.W. 45

Tajes, M. 85, 86, 88, 90
teaching assistants (TAs) 53, 54; language assistant (LA) programs differing from traditional 54–56
technology strategies: introduction to 12, 13; project-based language learning 13, 21–29; self-assessment and 10, 38, 44–49, 51, 52, 64, 65, 102; video-synchronous computer-mediated communication (VSCMC) 10, 13, 14, 19–23, 28, 29
Todd, R.W. 44
Topping, K. 60, 64, 65, 67, 69

UNC Charlotte: background of Japanese learning and circumstances in 6, 7; case of Japanese at 5, 6; particular problems for Japanese learners at 7–9; strategies to enhance student motivation for learning Japanese at 3–5, 9–11, *11*, 101–104

video-synchronous computer-mediated communication (VSCMC): advice for creating 19–21, 29, 30; conclusions 19; indications of success with 16–19; project-based language learning integrated with 21–26; Skype partner program case study in 14–16; tackling the poverty of opportunity problem through 13–21; theoretical motivation for, with native speakers 13, 14

Wiese, A.-M. 32, 33
Woo, Y. 14

Yang, N. 86
Yang, N.D. 44
Yang, Y.C. 13
year-end presentations 55, 67, 93–97, 99, 100
Youngs, B.L. 65, 67